KB243096

학습 진도표

본책은 오늘, 워크북은 내일! 부담되지 않은 분량을 정해서 꾸준히 공부하세요.

		학습 분량	학습일
Unit 1	1일차	☐ Mainbook	◯ 월 ◯ 일
	2일차	☐ Workbook	◯ 월 ◯ 일
Unit 2	3일차	☐ Main book	◯ 월 ◯ 일
	4일차	☐ Workbook	◯ 월 ◯ 일
Unit 3	5일차	☐ Main book	◯ 월 ◯ 일
	6일차	☐ Workbook	◯ 월 ◯ 일
Unit 4	7일차	☐ Main book	◯ 월 ◯ 일
	8일차	☐ Workbook	◯ 월 ◯ 일
Unit 5	9일차	☐ Main book	◯ 월 ◯ 일
	10일차	☐ Workbook	◯ 월 ◯ 일
Unit 6	11일차	☐ Main book	◯ 월 ◯ 일
	12일차	☐ Workbook	◯ 월 ◯ 일
Unit 7	13일차	☐ Main book	◯ 월 ◯ 일
	14일차	☐ Workbook	◯ 월 ◯ 일
Unit 8	15일차	☐ Main book	◯ 월 ◯ 일
	16일차	☐ Workbook	◯ 월 ◯ 일
Unit 9	17일차	☐ Main book	◯ 월 ◯ 일
	18일차	☐ Workbook	◯ 월 ◯ 일
Unit 10	19일차	☐ Main book	◯ 월 ◯ 일
	20일차	☐ Workbook	◯ 월 ◯ 일

		학습 분량	학습일
Unit 11	21일차	☐ Mainbook	◯ 월 ◯ 일
	22일차	☐ Workbook	◯ 월 ◯ 일
Unit 12	23일차	☐ Main book	◯ 월 ◯ 일
	24일차	☐ Workbook	◯ 월 ◯ 일
Unit 13	25일차	☐ Main book	◯ 월 ◯ 일
	26일차	☐ Workbook	◯ 월 ◯ 일
Unit 14	27일차	☐ Main book	◯ 월 ◯ 일
	28일차	☐ Workbook	◯ 월 ◯ 일
Unit 15	29일차	☐ Main book	◯ 월 ◯ 일
	30일차	☐ Workbook	◯ 월 ◯ 일
Unit 16	31일차	☐ Main book	◯ 월 ◯ 일
	32일차	☐ Workbook	◯ 월 ◯ 일
Unit 17	33일차	☐ Main book	◯ 월 ◯ 일
	34일차	☐ Workbook	◯ 월 ◯ 일
Unit 18	35일차	☐ Main book	◯ 월 ◯ 일
	36일차	☐ Workbook	◯ 월 ◯ 일
Unit 19	37일차	☐ Main book	◯ 월 ◯ 일
	38일차	☐ Workbook	◯ 월 ◯ 일
Unit 20	39일차	☐ Main book	◯ 월 ◯ 일
	40일차	☐ Workbook	◯ 월 ◯ 일

끊어 읽기로 빠르고 정확한 독해 완성하기

기적의 직독직해

120 words A

E2K 지음

길벗스쿨

기적의 직독직해: 120 words A
Miracle Series – Quick Reading and Understanding

초판 발행 · 2024년 12월 23일
초판 2쇄 발행 · 2025년 10월 1일

지은이 · E2K
발행인 · 이종원
발행처 · (주)길벗스쿨
출판사 등록일 · 2025년 5월 28일 | **주소** · 서울시 마포구 월드컵로 10길 56(서교동)
대표 전화 · 02)332-0931 | **팩스** · 02)322-3895
홈페이지 · www.gilbutschool.co.kr | **이메일** · gilbut@gilbut.co.kr

기획 및 책임편집 · 이경희(natura@gilbut.co.kr), 김소이 | **디자인** · 강은경, 신세진 | **제작** · 손일순
영업마케팅 · 문세연, 박선경, 구혜지, 박다슬 | **웹마케팅** · 박달님, 이재윤, 이지수, 나혜연 | **영업관리** · 정경화
독자지원 · 윤정아

전산편집 · 연디자인 | **표지삽화** · 오킹 | **본문삽화** · 천소
인쇄 · 대원문화사 | **제본** · 신정문화사 | **녹음** · 와이알미디어

∗ 잘못 만든 책은 구입한 서점에서 바꿔 드립니다.
∗ 이 책은 저작권법에 따라 보호받는 저작물이므로 무단전재와 무단복제를 금합니다.
　이 책의 전부 또는 일부를 이용하려면 반드시 사전에 저작권자와 길벗스쿨의 서면 동의를 받아야 합니다.

©E2K, 2024
ISBN 979-11-6406-846-3 64740 (길벗 도서번호 30622)
정가 16,000원

독자의 1초를 아껴주는 정성 길벗출판사
길벗 | IT실용서, IT/일반 수험서, IT전문서, 경제실용서, 취미실용서, 건강실용서, 자녀교육서
더퀘스트 | 인문교양서, 비즈니스서
길벗이지톡 | 어학단행본, 어학수험서
길벗스쿨 | 국어학습서, 수학학습서, 유아학습서, 어학학습서, 어린이교양서, 교과서

길벗스쿨 공식 카페 〈기적의 공부방〉 · cafe.naver.com/gilbutschool
인스타그램 / 카카오플러스친구 · @gilbutschool

기적의 직독직해

끊어 읽기를 통한 직독직해 연습은
영어 이해력, 읽기 속도, 정확성을 동시에 키워주는 필수 학습법입니다.

초등 저학년 단계에서는 주로 단어와 문맥을 통해 대략적인 의미를 유추하며 읽었다면, 고학년 시기에는 시험 영어에 대비해 문장을 정확하고 빠르게 이해하며 읽는 능력이 필요합니다. 문장을 의미 단위로 나누어 읽는 '끊어 읽기'를 연습하면 주어, 동사, 목적어 같은 문장 요소들을 자연스럽게 파악할 수 있으며, 길고 복잡한 문장도 더 쉽게 이해할 수 있게 됩니다. 이렇게 하면 문장을 앞뒤로 왔다갔다 하지 않고도 어순 그대로 읽으면서 즉시 이해하는 '직독직해' 실력이 길러집니다.

1 빠르고 정확한 문장 이해를 위한 끊어 읽기 훈련
의미 단위별 끊어 읽기를 통해 문장 전체를 정확히 이해하며 문장 구조를 파악하는 능력을 키웁니다.

2 다양한 장르의 흥미로운 글감을 골고루!
고학년 학생들의 흥미를 유발하는 뉴스와 지식, 전기문, 고전 동화, 창작 스토리 등 다양한 장르를 담았으며, 권당 160~200개의 연관 키워드를 함께 익힐 수 있도록 구성했습니다.

3 직독직해 실력을 높이는 핵심 문법과 문장 구조 알기
〈Grammar Point〉, 〈직독직해 Boost Up!〉 코너를 통해 주요 문법과 핵심 문장 구조를 익히고 실전에 활용할 수 있도록 합니다.

How to Study

Step 1
리딩 지문 읽기

지문 및 단어 듣기

주요 단어와 우리말 뜻을 보여줍니다.

먼저, 지문을 읽습니다. QR코드를 찍어서 원어민 음성을 들으며 눈으로 지문을 쫓아 읽습니다. 이 과정에서 주제와 대략적인 내용을 파악한 다음, 정확한 이해를 위해 문장 하나하나를 자세히 읽어 나갑니다.
낯선 어휘는 오른쪽의 단어 리스트를 통해 의미를 참고합니다.

Step 2
확인 테스트

지문 내용을 잘 이해했는지 문제를 통해 확인합니다.
A유형 서술된 문장이 옳은지 그른지를 판단하여 T 또는 F에 동그라미 하기
B유형 지문 내용을 토대로 질문에 알맞은 답을 고르기
C유형 알맞은 단어를 넣어 문장 완성하기

직독직해 Boost Up!

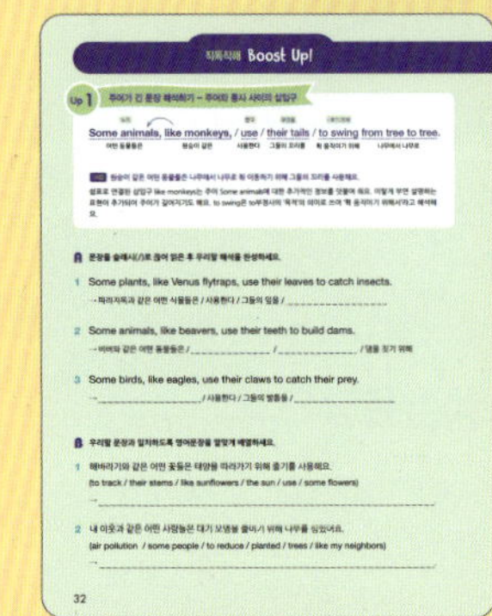

8가지 핵심 문장 구조를 끊어 읽는 보너스 Tip

직독직해를 위해 알아둬야 할 문장 해석법 8가지를 제공합니다. 문장 구조를 이해하여 단어 위치에 따라 어떤 의미로 해석해야 하는지를 익힐 수 있습니다.

길벗스쿨 e클래스

eclass.gilbut.co.kr
길벗스쿨 e클래스에서 내려 받으세요.

- MP3 바로 듣기 및 전체 다운로드
- 워크시트 5종 다운로드

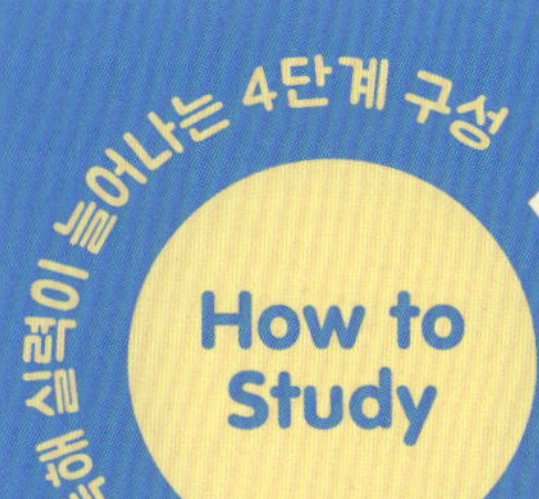

Step 3
끊어 읽기 연습

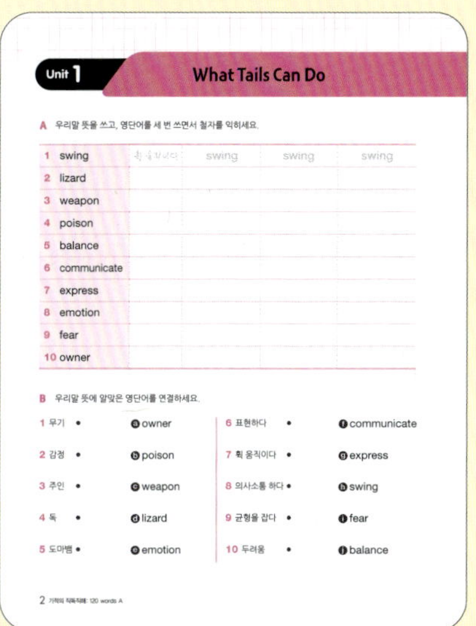

관용어구나 문형에 대한 간략한 설명으로 문장 이해를 돕습니다.

독해가 까다로운 문장에 대해 자세히 해설합니다. 문법과 구조를 이해하여 유사 문장을 해석할 수 있게 합니다.

정확한 문장 독해를 위해, 의미 단위로 단어들을 뭉쳐서 뜻을 파악하는 연습을 합니다.
/(슬래시)로 구분된 영어 어구와 그에 해당하는 우리말 뜻을 확인하며 다시 한 번 지문을 읽어 나갑니다. 빈칸을 채우면서 해석에 주의가 필요한 문장들의 뜻을 제대로 이해했는지 확인합니다.

Step 4
워크북 활동

본책 학습 후 워크북 풀이를 통해 어휘력 보강과 지문 복습을 합니다.
A유형 본책에서 다룬 필수 어휘를 따라 쓰며 뜻 익히기
B유형 우리말 뜻에 알맞은 영단어와 연결하기
C유형 단어 선택 문제를 풀며 지문을 다시 한 번 철저하게 복습하기

부가 학습자료

· 총정리 테스트 · 무료 워크시트 5종

단어 테스트

끊어 읽기 연습

딕테이션

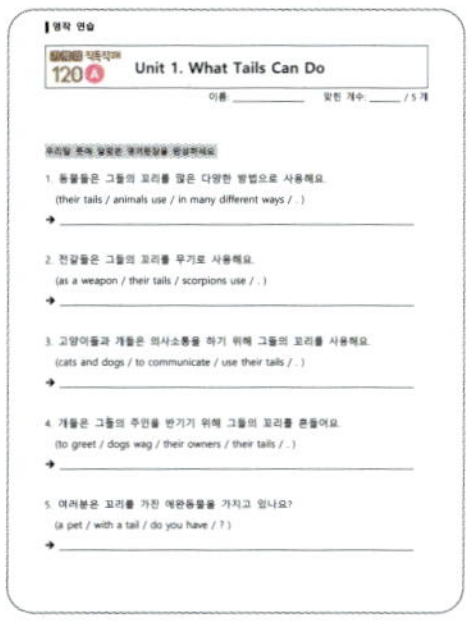

영작 연습

문장 해석

직독직해를 위한 가이드!

우리가 영어를 어렵게 느끼는 가장 큰 이유는 우리말과 영어의 서로 다른 어순 때문일 겁니다. 우리말은 '나는 물을 마신다'라는 어순이지만, 영어는 '나는 마신다 물을'로 우리말과 다른 어순을 갖기 때문이에요. 영어를 우리말 순서에 맞춰 해석하는 것은 좋지 않은 습관입니다. 영어 어순 그대로 읽어가며 바로바로 뜻을 파악하는 영어식 사고에 익숙해져야 해요. 그렇게 되면 리딩 속도가 빨라지는 것은 물론, 더욱 정확하고 완벽한 독해를 해낼 수 있습니다.

영어 어순대로 읽는 즉시 문장의 뜻을 이해하는 것, 즉 직독직해를 할 수 있으려면 단어들을 묶어서 하나의 의미 덩어리로 읽어낼 수 있어야 해요. 일명 '끊어 읽기' 연습을 통해 의미 단위로 구분하여 이해하는 힘을 기를 수 있습니다. 다음에 제시하는 기본 규칙을 적용하여 의미 단위로 끊어 읽는 연습을 해보세요. 많은 글을 읽으며 연습하다 보면 문장을 파악하는 감각이 저절로 생겨날 것입니다.

'주어＋동사'를 찾아서 해석해요.

영어 문장은 '누가'(주어)＋'행동한다'(동사)를 나타내는 단어들로 시작해요. 어디까지가 '누가'를 나타내고 어디까지 '행동한다'를 의미하는지 파악하는 게 무엇보다 중요합니다. '주어＋동사'를 찾아서 한 묶음으로 끊어 이해해 보세요.

예 The sun rises / in the east.
　 해가　　　　 뜬다

She washes / her hands.
그녀는 씻는다

Dorothy and her dog, Toto, follow / the yellow brick road.
도로시와 그녀의 개 '토토'는　　　　　　　 따라간다　　◀┈ 주어가 길어지는 경우도 있어요.

They will be waiting / for you.　　　◀┈ 동사구가 여러 단어로 이루어지기도 해요. (미래 진행형)
그들은　 기다리고 있을 것이다

The puppet was called / "Pinocchio."　　◀┈ 동사구가 여러 단어로 이루어지기도 해요.
그 인형은　　　　 불렸다　　　　　　　　　　　　 (수동태)

'주어+동사' 뒤에 명사가 올 때

'누가 ~한다'라는 말 뒤에는 보통 '무엇을'이란 말이 나옵니다.

예 **Jason ate / ice cream.**
제이슨은 먹었다　아이스크림을

Birds drink / water / every day.
새는 마신다　　　물을

be동사 뒤에 오는 '명사'는 신분이나 정체를 나타냅니다. 그래서 '주어+be동사+명사'는 주로 '주어는 (신분이) ~이다'로 이해하면 됩니다.

예 **My mom is / a nurse.**
우리 엄마는 ~이다　간호사

Mozart was / a genius musician.　　　…→ 명사 앞에 명사를 수식하는 말이 들어가기도 해요.
모짜르트는 ~였다　　천재 음악가

'주어+동사' 뒤에 형용사가 올 때

주어+동사 뒤에 형용사가 올 때는 주어의 상태가 어떠한지를 말해요. '누가 (기분이) 어떠하다' 또는 '무엇이 (상태가) 어떠하다'라고 해석합니다.

예 **Jane feels / happy.**
제인은 느낀다　행복한　　　　　　…→ 제인은 행복하다

This food smells / bad.
이 음식은 냄새 난다　　　안 좋은　　　…→ 이 음식은 안 좋은 냄새가 난다

My father is / sick / with the cold.
아빠는 ~이다　　　아픈　　　　　…→ 아빠는 아프다

'주어+동사' 뒤에 '전치사+명사'가 올 때

'어디에서'를 나타내는 덩어리들은 보통 '전치사+명사'로 이루어집니다. at, on, in, from 등이 대표적인 전치사예요.

예 **They danced / on the stage.**
그들은 춤췄다　　　무대에서

Amy came / from Chicago.
에이미는 왔다   시카고에서

Some animals live / in the desert.
몇몇 동물들이 산다   사막에

'전치사+명사' 덩어리가 '언제'를 나타내기도 합니다.

예 Deserts are cold / at night.
사막은 춥다   밤에

I have a test / on Monday.
나는 시험이 있다   월요일에

He gets up early / in the morning.
그는 일찍 일어난다   아침에

문장 중간에 'to+동사원형'이 올 때

주어+동사 외에 또 다른 동사가 문장 중간에 등장할 때가 있어요. 'to+동사원형' 형태의 덩어리들은 다양하게 해석될 수 있는데, 맥락에 따라 '~하기 위해서' 또는 '~하는 것', '~할/~하는'으로 해석됩니다.

예 I saved / some money / to help my friend.   ⋯to: ~하기 위해
나는 저축했다 돈을   내 친구를 돕기 위해

I will go / to the library / to borrow some books.   ⋯to: ~하기 위해
나는 갈 것이다   도서관에   책을 몇 권 빌리러

It is fun / to ride bicycles.   ⋯to: ~하는 것
재미있다   자전거를 타는 것은

I need some water / to drink.   ⋯to: ~할
나는 물이 필요하다   마실

'주어+동사' 뒤에 목적어가 두 개 올 때

주어+동사 뒤에 목적어가 두 개 올 때는 '…에게 ~을 한다'라는 의미로 해석하면 됩니다.

예 Mr. Brown teaches / us / English.
브라운 선생님은 가르친다   우리에게 영어를

I gave / Jane / a Christmas card / last Sunday.
나는 줬다   제인에게 성탄절 카드를

'주어+동사+목적어' 뒤에 목적어를 보충 설명하는 말이 올 때

주어+동사 뒤에 목적어 하나가 오는 것으로 그치지 않고, 목적어의 상태를 나타내는 단어가 같이 따라올 수 있어요. 이때는 '목적어를 ~하게 만든다/한다'라고 해석합니다.

- 예 **This book made / me / happy.**
  이 책은 만들었다　　　　　나를　행복하게

  They named / their baby / Sam.
  그들은 이름붙였다　　그들의 아기를　　샘이라고

접속사나 쉼표(,)를 기준으로 의미가 나뉠 때

그리고(and), 그러나(but), 왜냐하면(because), ~할 때(when) 등 다양한 의미의 접속사를 중심으로 의미가 나뉩니다. 문장을 읽어가다 내용의 흐름을 바꾸는 이러한 접속사가 나오면 끊어 읽기를 하세요.

- 예 **He came to the party / but she didn't.**
  그는 파티에 왔다　　　　　　　　하지만 그녀는 안 왔다

  My mom peeled the potatoes, / and I washed the lettuce.
  엄마가 감자를 벗겼다　　　　　　그리고 나는 상추를 씻었다

  Pam is worried / because her cat is ill.
  팸은 걱정한다　　　　왜냐하면 그녀의 고양이가 아프기 때문이다

문장 앞에 삽입구가 들어갈 때

주어+동사로 시작하기 전에 문장 앞에 삽입구가 오기도 합니다. 삽입구 뒤에 보통 쉼표(,)가 따라오기 때문에 주어+동사와 쉽게 구분할 수 있어요.

- 예 **One day, / I found an old sticker.**
  어느 날　　　　나는 오래된 스티커를 발견했다

  For example, / ants have three body parts.
  예를 들면　　　　　개미는 몸통이 세 부분으로 나누어져 있다

  Thanks to your help, / I could finish my homework.
  너의 도움 덕분에　　　　　내 숙제를 끝낼 수 있었어

Contents

What Tails Can Do

Animals use their tails in many different ways. Some animals, like monkeys, use their tails to swing from tree to tree. Some animals, like lizards, use their tails for self-defense. Scorpions use their tails as a weapon. It has poison in it. Fish use their tails to move through water. Kangaroos and squirrels use their tails to help themselves balance. Birds use their tails to help themselves fly in the sky.

Cats and dogs use their tails to communicate. They can use their tails to express many emotions such as fear and excitement. Dogs wag their tails to greet their owners.

Do you have a pet with a tail? If you do, how does the pet use its tail?

- **way** 방법, 방식
- **swing** 휙 움직이다
- **lizard** 도마뱀
- **self-defense** 자기 방어
- **scorpion** 전갈
- **weapon** 무기
- **poison** 독
- **themselves** 그들 자신
- **balance** 균형을 잡다
- **communicate** 의사소통을 하다
- **express** 표현하다
- **emotion** 감정
- **fear** 두려움
- **excitement** 흥분, 신남
- **wag** (꼬리를) 흔들다
- **greet** 인사하다
- **owner** 주인

Comprehension Check

 문장을 읽고 옳으면 T(True), 틀리면 F(False)에 동그라미 하세요.

1 Monkeys use their tails for self-defense.　　　　　**T / F**

2 Scorpions use their tails as a weapon.　　　　　**T / F**

3 Dogs use their tails to communicate.　　　　　**T / F**

 다음을 읽고 알맞은 답을 고르세요.

1 This passage is mainly about ________________.

　ⓐ animals' weapons

　ⓑ animals' tails

　ⓒ animals' communication

2 What animals use their tails to move through water?

　ⓐ Kangaroos

　ⓑ Squirrels

　ⓒ Fish

3 Why do dogs wag their tails?

　ⓐ To greet their owners

　ⓑ To swing from tree to tree

　ⓒ To balance themselves

 문장을 완성하는 단어를 써 넣으세요.

1 Some animals, like lizards, use their tails for __________.

2 Scorpions use their tails as a __________.

3 Cats and dogs use their tails to __________.

● 잘 읽고 이해했나요? 문장의 정확한 의미를 알아보세요.

1. Animals use / their tails / in many different ways.
동물들은 사용한다　　그들의 꼬리를　　　________________________

→ 여기서 like는 '~같은'이라는 뜻의 전치사예요.

2. Some animals, / like monkeys, / use their tails / to swing /
어떤 동물들은　　　　　원숭이 같은　　　　그들의 꼬리를 사용한다　　________

from tree to tree.
나무에서 나무로

→ like lizards는 some animals를 설명하기 위해 추가된 것이어서 앞뒤에 쉼표가 있어요.

3. Some animals, / like lizards, / use their tails / for self-defense.
어떤 동물들은　　　　　도마뱀 같은　　　　그들의 꼬리를 사용한다　　________________

→ 여기서 as는 '~로', '~로서'라는 뜻의 전치사예요.

4. Scorpions use / their tails / as a weapon.
전갈들은 사용한다　　그들의 꼬리를　　________________

5. It has poison / in it.
________________　　그 안에

6. Fish use / their tails / to move through water.
물고기들은 사용한다　그들의 꼬리를　　______________________________

〈help A B〉는 'A가 B하는 것을 돕다'
→ 라는 뜻이에요.

7. Kangaroos and squirrels use / their tails / to help themselves balance.
캥거루들과 다람쥐들은 사용한다　　　　그들의 꼬리를　　__________________________

8. Birds use / their tails / to help themselves fly / in the sky.
새들은 사용한다　그들의 꼬리를　__________________________　하늘에서

9. Cats and dogs use / their tails / to communicate.
고양이들과 개들은 사용한다　　그들의 꼬리를　　________________

10. They can use / their tails / to express / many emotions /
그들은 사용할 수 있다　　그들의 꼬리를　　표현하기 위해　　많은 감정들을

such as fear and excitement.

____

11. Dogs wag / their tails / to greet their owners.

개들은 흔든다　　　그들의 꼬리를　　_______________________________

12. Do you have / a pet with a tail?

여러분은 갖고 있나요?　　_______________________________

13. If you do, / how / does the pet use / its tail?

그렇다면　　　어떻게　　그 애완동물은 사용하는가?　　_______________

Grammar Point　목적을 나타내는 〈to 동사원형〉

본문 쏙　Some animals, like monkeys, use their tails to swing from tree to tree.

원숭이 같은 어떤 동물들은 나무에서 나무로 휙 이동하기 위해 꼬리를 사용한다.

to swing 같은 'to 동사원형' 형태를 'to부정사'라고 해요. to부정사는 문장 속에서 여러 가지 역할을 하는데, 예문에서 to swing은 '휙 이동하기 위해서'라는 뜻으로 쓰였어요. 이렇게 to부정사는 '~하기 위해서'라는 '목적'을 나타내기도 해요.

확인문제　**1**　We came here to meet you.

____

2　I went to the library to study.

____

Stay Healthy, Alpo

Yesterday morning, Alpo didn't eat or move. He had a runny nose and a cough. Dad and I took Alpo to the animal hospital. The vet said he had the flu. The vet also said to keep him inside and give him medicine for a few days. Dad said that since I was Alpo's big brother, it was my job to take good care of him.

Back at home, I put a clean blanket under Alpo. I gave him water and medicine. I fed him regularly. I kept him warm. I looked after Alpo all day. I fell asleep beside Alpo's house.

This morning, something wet woke me up. It was Alpo! Alpo looked great! I love you, Alpo!

- **runny nose** 콧물
- **cough** 기침
- **vet** 수의사
- **flu** 독감
- **medicine** 약
- **since** ~ 때문에
- **take care of** ~를 돌보다
- **blanket** 담요
- **fed** 먹이를 줬다 (feed 먹이를 주다)
- **regularly** 규칙적으로
- **look after** ~를 돌보다
- **beside** 옆에
- **wet** 젖은
- **woke up** 깨웠다 (wake up 깨우다)

16

Comprehension Check

A 문장을 읽고 옳으면 T(True), 틀리면 F(False)에 동그라미 하세요.

1 Alpo was sick because he got the flu.　　　　　　　**T / F**

2 The boy looked after Alpo all day.　　　　　　　　**T / F**

3 Alpo gave me water and medicine.　　　　　　　　**T / F**

B 다음을 읽고 알맞은 답을 고르세요.

1 This passage is mainly about ________________.

　ⓐ a boy and his dog

　ⓑ a boy and his dad

　ⓒ the animal hospital

2 What did the boy put under Alpo, back at home?

　ⓐ A wet towel　　　　ⓑ A clean blanket　　　　ⓒ Some medicine

3 What happened after the boy looked after Alpo all day?

　ⓐ The boy met his big brother.

　ⓑ The boy fell asleep beside Alpo's house.

　ⓒ The boy took some medicine.

C 문장을 완성하는 단어를 써 넣으세요.

1 Alpo had a __________ nose and a __________.

2 Dad said that since I was Alpo's big brother, it was my __________ to take good __________ of him.

3 This morning, something __________ woke me up.

Read and Understand

● 잘 읽고 이해했나요? 문장의 정확한 의미를 알아보세요.

1. Yesterday morning, / Alpo didn't eat or move.
어제 아침에

→ runny nose나 cough 같은 증상·병 이름 앞에는 주로 동사 have를 사용해요.

2. He had / a runny nose and a cough.
그는 갖고 있었다

3. Dad and I / took Alpo / to the animal hospital.
아빠와 나는　　　　　　　　　　동물 병원에

→ '독감에 걸리다'는 catch/get the flu라고도 해요.

4. The vet said / he had the flu.
수의사 선생님은 말씀하셨다

→ 〈give A B〉는 'A에게 B를 주다'라는 뜻이에요.

5. The vet also said / to keep him inside / and give him medicine /
수의사 선생님은 또한 말씀하셨다　그를 실내에 있게 하라고

for a few days.
며칠 동안

6. Dad said that / since I was Alpo's big brother, / it was my job /
아빠는 ~라고 말씀하셨다　내가 알포의 형이므로　　　　　　나의 일이다

to take good care of him.

7. Back at home, / I put a clean blanket / under Alpo.
집으로 돌아와서　　　　　　　　　　　　　　알포 밑에

8. I gave him / water and medicine.
　　　　　　　물과 약을

→ 〈keep A B〉는 'A를 B한 상태로 유지하다'라는 뜻이에요.

9. I fed him / regularly.　I kept him warm.
나는 그에게 먹이를 줬다　규칙적으로

10. I looked after / Alpo / all day.
나는 돌봤다　　　　알포를

fall asleep은 '잠들다'라는 뜻이에요.

11. I fell asleep / beside Alpo's house.
알포의 집 옆에서

something을 꾸며주는 형용사는 something 뒤에서 꾸며줘요.

12. This morning, / something wet / woke me up.　It was Alpo!
오늘 아침에　　　　　　　　　　　　　　나를 깨웠다　　　그것은 알포였다!

13. Alpo looked great!　I love you, Alpo!
사랑해, 알포야!

알아두면 문장이 쉽게
이해되는 그래머 포인트

이유를 나타내는 since

본문 쏙 Dad said that **since** I was Alpo's big brother, it was my job to take good care of him.
아빠는 내가 알포의 형이므로, 그를 잘 돌보는 것은 나의 일이라고 말씀하셨다.

이 문장에서 since는 '~이므로, 때문에'라는 뜻으로 I was Alpo's big brother.라는 문장과 It was my job to take good care of him.이라는 문장을 연결해 주는 접속사로 쓰였어요. 이유를 나타내는 접속사 because(~ 때문에)와 같은 뜻이랍니다.

확인문제 **1** Since I have no money, I can't buy a cup.

2 Since we are students, we need to study hard.

Florence Nightingale

In 1845, Florence Nightingale became a nurse in England. Years later, she read about the poor treatment of sick and injured soldiers in the Crimean War. She went to Crimea and found dirty and crowded hospitals. She knew that more soldiers died from diseases than from injuries in the war.

She worked hard to clean the hospital and take care of the injured soldiers. Florence walked around the hospital in the evenings, carrying a lamp and checking on the injured soldiers. For this reason, many soldiers called her "The Lady with the Lamp." Thanks to her, fewer soldiers died from diseases.

Florence established the Nightingale School for nurses. She was the best nurse in the world.

- **England** 영국
- **read** 읽었다
  (read 읽다)
- **treatment** 치료
- **injured** 부상당한
- **soldier** 군인
- **the Crimean War** 크림 전쟁
- **Crimea** 크림 반도
- **crowded** 붐비는
- **injury** 부상, 상처
- **lamp** 램프, 등
- **check on** ~을 확인하다
- **reason** 이유
- **fewer** 더 적은
- **establish** 설립하다

Comprehension Check

A 문장을 읽고 옳으면 T(True), 틀리면 F(False)에 동그라미 하세요.

1 Florence Nightingale was born in 1845. T / F

2 More soldiers died from diseases than from injuries in the war. T / F

3 Florence established the Nightingale School for soldiers. T / F

B 다음을 읽고 알맞은 답을 고르세요.

1 This passage is mainly about ________________.

   ⓐ the Crimean War　　　　**ⓑ** Florence Nightingale　　　　**ⓒ** diseases

2 Why did Florence work hard at the hospital in Crimea?

   ⓐ To meet the lady with the lamp

   ⓑ To be a nurse

   ⓒ To take care of the injured soldiers

3 Why did the soldiers call Florence "The Lady with the Lamp"?

   ⓐ Because she established a school for nurses.

   ⓑ Because she fixed lamps in the evenings.

   ⓒ Because she checked on the injured soldiers while carrying a lamp in the evenings.

C 문장을 완성하는 단어를 써 넣으세요.

1 In 1845, Florence Nightingale __________ a nurse in England.

2 Years later, she read about the _________ treatment of sick and _________ soldiers in the Crimean War.

3 Florence walked around the hospital in the evenings, __________ a lamp and __________ on the injured soldiers.

Read and Understand

● 잘 읽고 이해했나요? 문장의 정확한 의미를 알아보세요.

→ 연도 앞에는 전치사 in을 사용해요.

1. In 1845, / Florence Nightingale / became a nurse / in England.
1845년에　　　플로렌스 나이팅게일은　　　　　　　　　　　　　영국에서

→ 여기서 poor는 '가난한'이 아닌 '부족한, 열악한'이라는 뜻이에요.

2. Years later, / she read / about the poor treatment / of sick and injured
몇 년 후에　　　그녀는 읽었다　　　　　　　　　　　　　　　병들고 부상당한 병사들의

soldiers / in the Crimean War.
크림 전쟁에서

3. She went to Crimea / and found / dirty and crowded hospitals.
그녀는 크림 반도에 갔다　　　　그리고 발견했다

→ that~war가 knew의 목적어이고, that은 목적절을 이끄는 역할을 해요.

4. She knew / that more soldiers died / from diseases /
그녀는 알았다　　더 많은 군인들이 죽는다는 것을　　　질병으로 인해

than from injuries in the war.

5. She worked hard / to clean the hospital / and take care of /
그녀는 열심히 일했다　　　　병원을 청소하기 위해　　　　　　　그리고 돌보기 위해

the injured soldiers.

evening에 s가 붙어 있으므로
→ '매일 저녁'을 뜻해요.

6. Florence walked around / the hospital / in the evenings, /
플로렌스는 돌아다녔다　　　　　　　　병원을　　　　　　　저녁마다

carrying a lamp / and checking on / the injured soldiers.
　　　　　　　　　　　　그리고 확인하며　　　　부상당한 군인들을

→ 〈call A B〉는 'A를 B라고 부르다'라는 뜻이에요.

7. For this reason, / many soldiers called her / "The Lady with the Lamp."
　　　　　　　　　많은 군인들이 그녀를 불렀다　　　　　"램프를 든 여인"이라고

→ Thanks to...는 '~ 덕분에'라는 뜻이에요.

8. Thanks to her, / fewer soldiers / died from diseases.
그녀 덕분에　　　　　　　　　　　질병으로 죽었다

9. Florence established / the Nightingale School / for nurses.

플로렌스는 설립했다 　　　　　나이팅게일 학교를 　　　　　________________

10. She was the best nurse / in the world.

________________________________　세상에서

Grammar Point　설명을 보충하는 현재분사

본문 쏙　Florence walked around the hospital in the evenings, carrying a lamp and checking on the injured soldiers.

플로렌스는 저녁마다 램프를 들고 부상당한 군인들을 확인하며 병원을 돌아다녔다.

carrying과 checking은 동사에 -ing를 붙인 '현재분사'예요. 예문에서 carrying은 '들고서', checking은 '확인하면서'라는 뜻으로 주어인 Florence의 행동을 좀 더 자세히 설명하고 있어요. 이렇게 현재분사는 '~하면서', '~하고서'라는 뜻으로 쓰이면서 주어의 상태나 행위를 보충 설명하기도 한답니다.

확인문제　**1**　The teacher looked around the classroom, checking on the students.

2　Peter jogged in the mornings, wearing only his shorts.

The Lion and the Mouse

A little mouse began climbing up a brown hill and slid down. But the hill was a sleeping lion's back! Bothered by the mouse, the lion woke up. The angry lion caught the mouse between his claws. "Please let me go. Then I'll come back and help you someday," said the mouse.

The lion laughed, "You are so tiny! How can a tiny mouse help me?" But the lion let the little mouse go because he could laugh thanks to the mouse.

The next day, the lion was caught in a trap. The mouse came to him and began to cut the rope with his teeth. Finally, the lion could get out of the trap.

"Dear friend, you saved me after all. Thank you," said the lion.

"I'm glad I could help you," said the mouse.

- **began** 시작했다 (begin 시작하다)
- **climb up** ~에 오르다
- **hill** 언덕
- **slid** 미끄러졌다 (slide 미끄러지다)
- **back** 등
- **bother** 방해하다
- **caught** 잡았다 (catch 잡다)
- **claw** (동물의) 발톱
- **someday** 언젠가
- **trap** 덫
- **rope** 밧줄
- **teeth** 이빨들 (tooth 이, 이빨)
- **save** 구하다
- **after all** 결국

Comprehension Check

A 문장을 읽고 옳으면 T(True), 틀리면 F(False)에 동그라미 하세요.

1 A little mouse climbed up and slid down a lion's back.   **T / F**

2 The lion caught the mouse between his claws.   **T / F**

3 The lion saved the mouse from a trap.   **T / F**

B 다음을 읽고 알맞은 답을 고르세요.

1 What can you learn from this story?

   ⓐ Everything can be helpful in different ways.

   ⓑ It is better to be good at only one thing.

   ⓒ Don't fight with little friends.

2 The next day after he let the mouse go, what happened to the lion?

   ⓐ He climbed up a brown hill.

   ⓑ He caught the mouse between his claws.

   ⓒ He was caught in a trap.

3 How did the mouse help the lion get out of the trap?

   ⓐ The mouse cut the rope with his feet.

   ⓑ The mouse cut the rope with his tail.

   ⓒ The mouse cut the rope with his teeth.

C 문장을 완성하는 단어를 써 넣으세요.

1 A little mouse began ___________ up a brown hill and slid down.

2 ___________ by the mouse, the lion woke up.

3 But the lion ___________ the little mouse go because he could ___________ thanks to the mouse.

● 잘 읽고 이해했나요? 문장의 정확한 의미를 알아보세요.

〈began + -ing〉는 '~하기 시작했다'로 해석해요.

1. A little mouse / began climbing up / a brown hill / and slid down.
작은 쥐가 _______________________ 갈색 언덕을 그리고 미끄러져 내려왔다

2. But / the hill was / a sleeping lion's back!
하지만 그 언덕은 ~였다 _______________________

3. Bothered / by the mouse, / the lion woke up.
방해를 받아서 쥐에 의해 _______________________

4. The angry lion / caught the mouse / between his claws.
화가 난 사자는 쥐를 잡았다 _______________________

let me go는 '내가 가게 하다', 즉 '나를 놓아 주다'라는 뜻이에요.

5. "Please let me go. / Then I'll come back / and help you / someday," /
_______________________ 그러면 제가 다시 와서 당신을 도울게요 언젠가

said the mouse.
쥐가 말했다

6. The lion laughed, / "You are so tiny! / How can a tiny mouse help me?"
사자는 웃었다 너는 너무 작아 _______________________

7. But the lion / let the little mouse go / because he could laugh /
하지만 그 사자는 _______________________ 그가 웃을 수 있었기 때문에

thanks to the mouse.
쥐 덕분에

was caught는 수동태로 '잡혔다'라는 뜻이에요.

8. The next day, / the lion was caught / in a trap.
다음 날 _______________________ 덫에

9. The mouse came to him / and began to cut / the rope / with his teeth.
쥐가 그에게 왔다 그리고 끊기 시작했다 밧줄을 _______________________

10. Finally, / the lion could get out / of the trap.
마침내   덫에서

11. "Dear friend, / you saved me / after all. / Thank you," / said the lion.
사랑하는 친구야   결국   고맙구나   사자가 말했다

12. "I'm glad / I could help you," / said the mouse.
저는 기뻐요   쥐가 말했다

Grammar Point — **begin** + 동명사 / **to** 부정사

본문 쏙 A little mouse began climbing up a brown hill.
작은 쥐가 갈색 언덕에 오르기 시작했다.

The mouse came to him and began to cut the rope with his teeth.
쥐가 그에게 와서 이빨로 밧줄을 끊기 시작했다.

'~하기 시작하다'라고 할 때 begin 뒤에는 동명사(동사+-ing)나 to 부정사(to+동사원형)를 모두 사용할 수 있어요. began climbing(오르기 시작했다) 대신 began to climb이라고 해도 되고, began to cut(끊기 시작했다) 대신 began cutting이라고 해도 된답니다.

확인문제 **1** He began taking a shower.

2 I began to sing a song.

the oldest bridge in Turkey

Tower Bridge in London

Golden Gate Bridge in San Francisco

Bridges Around the World

People build bridges over rivers, roads, and railroads. This way, people or vehicles can cross from one side to the other.

There are some famous bridges. The Golden Gate Bridge is one of these bridges. It is a landmark in San Francisco, California. Many tourists like to take pictures of it. Tower Bridge, in London, is another famous bridge in the world. It goes across the River Thames. In Australia, vehicles and trains as well as bicycles and pedestrians cross the Sydney Harbor Bridge.

The world's longest bridge is the Danyang-Kunshan Grand Bridge in China. It opened in June 2011. It's almost 165 kilometers long. The oldest bridge is in Turkey. It was built in 850 B.C., and it is still in use today.

- **bridge** 다리
- **over** ~ 위로
- **railroad** 철로
- **vehicle** 차량
- **cross** 건너다
- **famous** 유명한
- **landmark** 랜드마크
- **tourist** 관광객
- **take a picture of** ~의 사진을 찍다
- **another** 또 다른
- **across** 가로질러
- **as well as** ~뿐만 아니라
- **pedestrian** 보행자
- **B.C.**(before Christ) 기원전

Comprehension Check

A 문장을 읽고 옳으면 T(True), 틀리면 F(False)에 동그라미 하세요.

1 People build bridges over houses or buildings.　　　**T / F**

2 The Golden Gate Bridge is a famous bridge.　　　**T / F**

3 The world's longest bridge is Tower Bridge.　　　**T / F**

B 다음을 읽고 알맞은 답을 고르세요.

1 This passage is mainly about _______________.

　ⓐ bridges in the USA

　ⓑ bridges around the world

　ⓒ long bridges

2 What do people build over rivers to cross from one side to the other?

　ⓐ Railroads　　　　ⓑ Vehicles　　　　ⓒ Bridges

3 Where is the oldest bridge which is still in use today?

　ⓐ In the USA　　　　ⓑ In Turkey　　　　ⓒ In China

C 문장을 완성하는 단어를 써 넣으세요.

1 This way, people or vehicles can cross from one __________ to the other.

2 In Australia, vehicles and trains as __________ as bicycles and __________ cross the Sydney Harbor Bridge.

3 The world's __________ bridge is the Danyang-Kunshan Grand Bridge in China.

● 잘 읽고 이해했나요? 문장의 정확한 의미를 알아보세요.

over는 '한쪽에서 다른 쪽으로 가로질러 위로'라는 뜻을 담고 있어요.

1. People build bridges / over / rivers, roads, and railroads.
_____________________   ~ 위로   강들, 도로들, 그리고 철길들

the other는 '둘 중의 다른 하나'를 뜻해요.

2. This way, / people or vehicles / can cross / from one side to the other.
이 방법으로   사람들이나 차들은   건너갈 수 있다 _____________________

3. There are / some famous bridges.
있다 _____________________

bridges가 복수이므로 this가 아니라 these를 써야 해요.

4. The Golden Gate Bridge / is one of these bridges.
금문교는 _____________________

landmark(랜드마크)는 멀리서 보고 위치 파악에 도움이 되는 대형 건물 같은 것을 말해요.

5. It is a landmark / in San Francisco, / California.
_____________________   샌프란시스코에서   캘리포니아 주의

it은 the Golden Gate Bridge를 말해요.

6. Many tourists like / to take pictures / of it.
많은 관광객들은 좋아한다 _____________________   그것의

7. Tower Bridge, / in London, / is another famous bridge / in the world.
타워 브리지는   런던에 있는 _____________________   세계에서

8. It goes across / the River Thames.
_____________________   템스 강을

9. In Australia, / vehicles and trains / as well as bicycles and pedestrians /
호주에서는   차들과 기차들도 _____________________

cross / the Sydney Harbor Bridge.
건넌다   시드니 하버 브리지를

10. The world's longest bridge / is the Danyang-Kunshan Grand Bridge /
_____________________   단양-쿤산 대교이다

in China.
중국에 있는

11. It opened / in June 2011.

그것은 개통했다 ________________

12. It's almost 165 kilometers long.

____

13. The oldest bridge / is in Turkey.

________________ 터키에 있다

was built는 수동태로서 '지어졌다'라는 뜻이에요.

14. It was built / in 850 B.C., / and it is still in use / today.

________________ 기원전 850년에 　그리고 그것은 여전히 사용되고 있다　오늘날

Grammar Point　**A as well as B**

본문 쏙 In Australia, vehicles and trains <u>as well as</u> bicycles and pedestrians cross the Sydney Harbor Bridge.

호주에서는 자전거들과 보행자들뿐만 아니라 차들과 기차들도 시드니 하버 브리지를 건넌다.

A as well as B는 'B뿐만 아니라 A도'라는 뜻이에요. 즉, as well as 뒤에 언급한 내용인 bicycles and pedestrians(자전거들과 보행자들)뿐만 아니라 앞에 나오는 vehicles and trains(차들과 기차들)도 다리를 건넌다는 뜻이에요.

확인문제 **1** I want to learn Chinese as well as English.

____

2 The truck carries soil as well as rocks.

____

Up 1 주어가 긴 문장 해석하기 – 주어와 동사 사이의 삽입구

누가   한다   무엇을   ~하기 위해

Some animals, like monkeys, / use / their tails / to swing from tree to tree.

어떤 동물들은   원숭이 같은   사용한다   그들의 꼬리를   휙 움직이기 위해   나무에서 나무로

해설 원숭이 같은 어떤 동물들은 나무에서 나무로 휙 이동하기 위해 그들의 꼬리를 사용해요.

쉼표로 연결된 삽입구 like monkeys는 주어 Some animals에 대한 추가적인 정보를 덧붙여 줘요. 이렇게 부연 설명하는 표현이 추가되어 주어가 길어지기도 해요. to swing은 to부정사의 '목적'의 의미로 쓰여 '휙 움직이기 위해서'라고 해석해요.

A 문장을 슬래시(/)로 끊어 읽은 후 우리말 해석을 완성하세요.

1 Some plants, like Venus flytraps, use their leaves to catch insects.

→ 파리지옥과 같은 어떤 식물들은 / 사용한다 / 그들의 잎을 / _______________________

2 Some animals, like beavers, use their teeth to build dams.

→ 비버와 같은 어떤 동물들은 / _________________ / _________________ / 댐을 짓기 위해

3 Some birds, like eagles, use their claws to catch their prey.

→ _____________________ / 사용한다 / 그들의 발톱을 / _____________________

B 우리말 문장과 일치하도록 영어문장을 알맞게 배열하세요.

1 해바라기와 같은 어떤 꽃들은 태양을 따라가기 위해 줄기를 사용해요.

(to track / their stems / like sunflowers / the sun / use / some flowers)

→ ____.

2 내 이웃과 같은 어떤 사람들은 대기 오염을 줄이기 위해 나무를 심었어요.

(air pollution / some people / to reduce / planted / trees / like my neighbors)

→ ____.

이렇게 끊어 읽으면 직독직해가 술술!

Up 2 목적어가 긴 문장 해석하기 – 동명사구

누가　　　　　한다　　　　　　　무엇을

A little mouse / began / climbing up a brown hill.
작은 쥐 한 마리가　　　시작했다　　　　갈색 언덕을 오르기를

해설 작은 쥐 한 마리가 갈색 언덕을 오르기 시작했어요.

'주어+동사+목적어' 구조의 3형식 문장이에요. 동사 began의 목적어로 동명사 climbing(오르기, 오르는 것)을 썼어요. '동명사'는 동사에 -ing가 붙여진 것으로 명사처럼 쓰여요. 이 문장에서는 '갈색 언덕을 오르는 것(climbing up)을 시작했다'고 해석해요.

🅐 문장을 슬래시(/)로 끊어 읽은 후 우리말 해석을 완성하세요.

1 The young boy began reading a thick book.

→ 어린 소년이 / ________________ / 두꺼운 책 읽기를

2 A smart monkey began learning how to play the guitar.

→ 똑똑한 원숭이는 / 시작했다 / ________________________

3 My older sister began cleaning her closet.

→ 나의 언니는 / ________________ / ________________________

🅑 우리말 문장과 일치하도록 영어문장을 알맞게 배열하세요.

1 작은 새 한 마리가 새 둥지를 짓기 시작했다.

(building / a new nest / started / a small bird)

→ ____.

2 한 나이 든 여인이 아름다운 풍경을 그리기 시작했다.

(began / an old woman / a beautiful landscape / painting)

→ ____.

Fun to Learn

Our teacher, Mr. Watson, brought many pictures of sea animals to class. He put the pictures on the board and started to name them. An eel, cuttlefish, lobster, shrimp, clam, jellyfish, swordfish, seahorse, whale, sea lion, and so on. We knew some of their names, but it was hard to remember all of them.

Mr. Watson told our class fun facts about each sea animal. Giant cuttlefish have green blood. Lobsters have blue blood and they live up to 100 years. Shrimps can only swim backwards. Electric eels can light up ten electric bulbs.

These fun facts let us identify the animals easily. They were also fun to learn!

- **brought** 가져왔다
  (bring 가져오다)
- **class** 학급, 수업
- **board** 칠판, 판자
- **eel** 장어
- **cuttlefish** 갑오징어
- **lobster** 바닷가재
- **shrimp** 새우
- **clam** 조개
- **jellyfish** 해파리
- **swordfish** 황새치
- **seahorse** 해마
- **sea lion** 바다사자
- **backwards** 뒤로
- **electric** 전기의
- **light up** 밝히다
- **bulb** 전구
- **identify** 알아보다

Comprehension Check

A 문장을 읽고 옳으면 T(True), 틀리면 F(False)에 동그라미 하세요.

1 They're studying sea animals in the class.　　　　　　**T / F**

2 The students watched the sea animals on the TV program.　　**T / F**

3 Shrimps can only swim backwards.　　　　　　　　**T / F**

B 다음을 읽고 알맞은 답을 고르세요.

1 This passage is mainly about ________________.

　ⓐ fishermen

　ⓑ sea lions

　ⓒ sea animals

2 Which sea animals have green blood?

　ⓐ Jellyfish

　ⓑ Lobsters

　ⓒ Giant cuttlefish

3 What is a fact about electric eels?

　ⓐ They can light up ten electric bulbs.

　ⓑ They can only swim backwards.

　ⓒ Thy can live up to 100 years.

C 문장을 완성하는 단어를 써 넣으세요.

1 Mr. Watson brought many __________ of sea animals to class.

2 We knew some of their names, but it was hard to __________ all of them.

3 __________ have blue blood and they live up to 100 years.

Read and Understand

● 잘 읽고 이해했나요? 문장의 정확한 의미를 알아보세요.

1. Our teacher, Mr. Watson, brought / many pictures of sea animals / to class.

우리의 왓슨 선생님은 가져오셨다 　　　　　　　　　　　　　　　　　　　　　　수업에

여기서 name은 '이름을 말하다'라는 동사로 쓰였어요.

2. He put the pictures / on the board / and started / to name them.

그는 그 사진들을 붙였다　　　　칠판 위에　　　　그리고 시작했다

3. An eel, cuttlefish, lobster, shrimp, clam, jellyfish, swordfish, seahorse,

장어, 갑오징어, 바닷가재, 새우, 조개, 해파리, 황새치, 해마,

and so on은 '기타 등등'이라는 뜻이에요.

whale, sea lion, / and so on.

고래, 바다사자

4. We knew / some of their names, / but it was hard /

우리는 알았다　　　그것들의 이름 중 몇 개를　　　　　　하지만 어려웠다

to remember all of them.

(tell A B)는 'A에게 B를 말하다'라는 뜻이에요.

5. Mr. Watson told / our class / fun facts / about each sea animal.

왓슨 선생님은 말해 주셨다　　　우리 반에게　　　재미있는 사실들을

6. Giant cuttlefish have / green blood.

대왕 갑오징어들은 가지고 있다

up to는 '~까지'라는 뜻이에요.

7. Lobsters have / blue blood / and they live / up to 100 years.

바닷가재들은 가지고 있다　　파란색 피를　　　　그리고 그들은 산다

8. Shrimps can / only swim backwards.

새우들은 ~할 수 있다

light up은 '불을 켜다, 밝히다'라는 뜻이에요.

9. Electric eels can light up / ten electric bulbs.

　　　　　　　　　　　　　　　　　10개의 전구들을

10. These fun facts / let us identify / the animals / easily.

이런 재미있는 사실들은 ___________________ 그 동물들을 쉽게

11. They were also fun / to learn!

___________________ 배우기

Grammar Point | **가주어와 진주어**

본문 쏙 It was hard to remember all of them.

그것들 모두를 기억하는 것은 어려웠다.

이 문장에서 주어는 무엇일까요? 언뜻 보기에는 맨 앞에 있는 It이 주어인 것 같지만, '진주어(진짜 주어)'는 to remember all of them(그것들 모두를 기억하는 것은)이에요. 그런데 주어가 길다 보니 이렇게 뒤로 보내고, 주어 자리에 It을 대신 쓴 겁니다. 이렇게 쓰인 It을 '가주어(가짜 주어)'라고 해요.

확인문제 **1** It is fun to play basketball.

2 It was hard to bake cookies.

A Legendary Filmmaker

Have you seen the movies *Jaws*, *E.T.*, and *Jurassic Park*? Steven Spielberg directed all of these movies. He produced many of the biggest Hollywood blockbusters over the last 40 years. He used various themes and genres such as science fiction, humanism, and adventure in his films. Spielberg's films contained active and fantastic scenes. Audiences were very impressed with his movies and had fun watching them.

Steven Spielberg was born in Ohio, USA in 1946. From a young age, he had a big imagination and was full of curiosity. He filmed his first movie at the age of twelve. It was a hit with his family and friends. These days, Spielberg still works hard to make great movies. He loves his job and said, "I dream for a living."

- **direct** 감독하다
- **produce** 제작하다
- **blockbuster** 블록버스터
- **various** 다양한
- **theme** 주제
- **genre** 장르
- **science fiction** 공상 과학 영화[소설]
- **humanism** 인본주의
- **adventure** 모험
- **film** 영화; 촬영하다
- **contain** 담고 있다
- **active** 활동적인
- **fantastic** 환상적인
- **scene** 장면
- **audience** 관중, 청중
- **impressed** 감명[감동]을 받은
- **imagination** 상상
- **curiosity** 호기심
- **dream** 꿈; 꿈을 꾸다

Comprehension Check

A 문장을 읽고 옳으면 T(True), 틀리면 F(False)에 동그라미 하세요.

1 Steven Spielberg produced many of the biggest Hollywood blockbusters.　　**T / F**

2 Spielberg loved acting and making short songs.　　**T / F**

3 Spielberg used various genres in his films.　　**T / F**

B 다음을 읽고 알맞은 답을 고르세요.

1 This passage is mainly about ________________.

ⓐ Steven Spielberg

ⓑ blockbusters

ⓒ Hollywood

2 The movies *Jaws, E.T.,* and *Jurassic Park* were big hits. They are called
"________________."

ⓐ themes　　　　ⓑ blockbusters　　　　ⓒ adventures

3 At what age did he film his first movie?

ⓐ At twelve　　　　ⓑ At thirteen　　　　ⓒ At twenty

C 문장을 완성하는 단어를 써 넣으세요.

1 Audiences were very __________ with his movies and had __________ watching them.

2 From a young age, he had a big imagination and was full of __________.

3 He loves his job and said, "I __________ for a living."

Read and Understand

● 잘 읽고 이해했나요? 문장의 정확한 의미를 알아보세요.

1. Have you seen / the movies *Jaws*, *E.T.*, and *Jurassic Park*?
_______________   영화 죠스, E.T., 그리고 쥬라기 공원을

all of는 '~의 전부', '모든 ~'라는 뜻이에요.

2. Steven Spielberg directed / all of these movies.
스티븐 스필버그는 감독했다   _______________

blockbuster(블록버스터)는 '크게 성공한 책이나 영화'를 가리켜요.

3. He produced / many of the biggest Hollywood blockbusters /
그는 제작했다   할리우드에서 가장 크게 성공한 영화들 중 많은 수를

여기서 over는 '~ 이상', '~ 넘게'라는 뜻으로 쓰였어요.

over the last 40 years.
____

4. He used / various themes and genres /
그는 사용했다   다양한 주제들과 장르들을

such as는 '~와 같은'이란 뜻이에요.

such as science fiction, humanism, and adventure / in his films.
_______________   그의 영화에

5. Spielberg's films / contained / active and fantastic scenes.
스필버그의 영화들은   담고 있었다   _______________

be impressed with는 '~에 감명 받다'라는 뜻이에요.

6. Audiences were very impressed / with his movies /
_______________   그의 영화들에

and had fun watching them.
그리고 그것들을 보며 재미있어 했다

7. Steven Spielberg / was born / in Ohio, USA / in 1946.
스티븐 스필버그는   _______________   미국 오하이오 주에서   1946년에

8. From a young age, / he had a big imagination / and was full of
어린 시절부터   _______________   그리고 호기심으로 가득 차 있었다

curiosity.

9. He filmed his first movie / at the age of twelve.

_______________________ 열두 살에

10. It was a hit / with his family and friends.

_______________ 그의 가족과 친구들에게

11. These days, / Spielberg still works hard / to make great movies.

요즘　　　　　　　스필버그는 여전히 열심히 일한다　　　　_______________________

12. He loves his job / and said, / "I dream for a living."

그는 그의 일을 사랑한다　　　그리고 말했다　　_______________________

for a living은 '먹고 살기 위해'라고 해석해요.

Grammar Point **Have you + 과거분사?**

본문 쏙 **Have you seen** the movies *Jaws*, *E.T.*, and *Jurassic Park*?
영화 죠스, E.T., 그리고 쥬라기 공원을 본 적 있나요?

Have you seen...?은 '~을 본 적이 있나요?'라는 뜻이에요. 이렇게 과거부터 지금까지의 경험을 물을 때는 Did you see...?가 아니라 Have you seen...?이라고 물어요. Have you heard...?(~을 들어 본 적이 있나요?), Have you tried...?(~을 해 본 적이 있나요?)처럼 〈Have you + 과거분사?〉 형태는 '~해 본 적이 있나요?'라는 뜻의 경험을 묻는 표현이에요.

확인문제 **1** Have you seen my umbrella?

2 Have you heard about the new student?

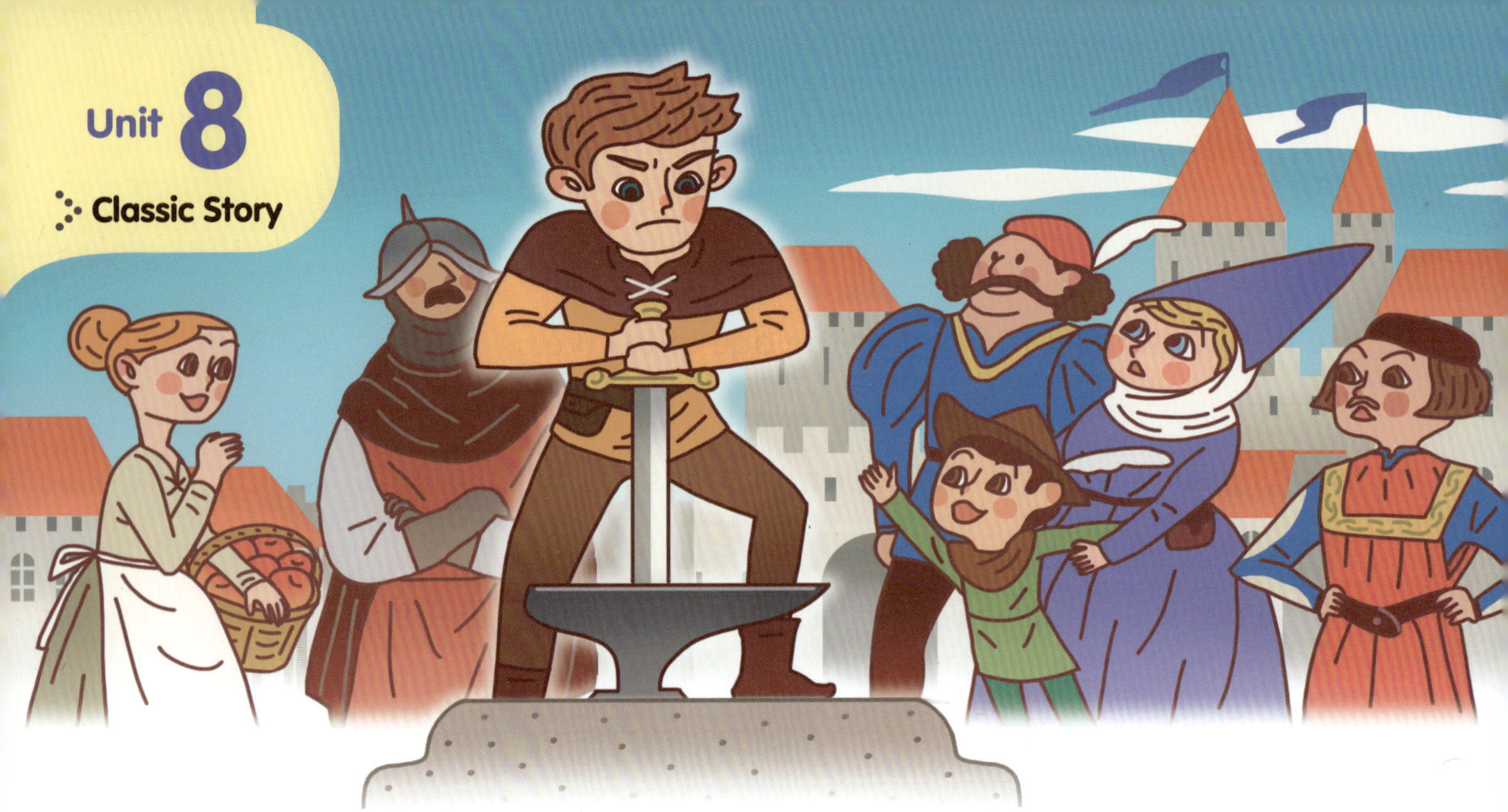

The Sword in the Stone

There was a sword in a large stone. These words were on the stone: "ONLY THE KING CAN TAKE THE SWORD FROM THE STONE." Every knight tried to pull the sword out of the stone. They pulled and pulled, but nobody could pull it out of the stone.

There was a big tournament in the country. Many knights came and fought on horses with swords in their hands. Arthur, a 15-year-old boy, wanted to fight with the other knights, too. But he didn't have a sword.

Arthur went to the stone. He took the sword in his hand and pulled. It came out of the stone easily. There was a crowd gathered around Arthur. The crowd cheered, and Arthur was crowned King of England.

- **sword** 검
- **word** 말, 글
- **stone** 돌
- **knight** (중세의) 기사
- **pull** 뽑다, 당기다
- **nobody** 아무도 ~않다
- **tournament** 마상시합, 토너먼트
- **country** 나라
- **fought** 싸웠다
- **fight** 싸우다
- **crowd** 군중
- **gather** 모이다
- **cheer** 환호하다
- **crown** 왕위에 앉히다

Comprehension Check

A 문장을 읽고 옳으면 T(True), 틀리면 F(False)에 동그라미 하세요.

1 There was a sword in a large case.　　　　　　　　　**T / F**

2 Only the knight could take the sword from the stone.　　**T / F**

3 At fifteen years old, Arthur pulled the sword from the stone.　**T / F**

B 다음을 읽고 알맞은 답을 고르세요.

1 This passage is mainly about _________________.

   ⓐ the sword in the stone

   ⓑ the knights' swords

   ⓒ the Knights of England

2 Knights came and fought on horses with swords in the _________________.

   ⓐ war

   ⓑ festival

   ⓒ tournament

3 What happened to Arthur after he pulled the sword out of the stone?

   ⓐ He joined a big tournament.

   ⓑ He became the king of England.

   ⓒ He became a knight for the king.

C 문장을 완성하는 단어를 써 넣으세요.

1 "Only the __________ can take the sword from the stone."

2 Every knight tried to __________ the sword out of the stone.

3 Arthur was __________ King of England.

● 잘 읽고 이해했나요? 문장의 정확한 의미를 알아보세요.

1. There was a sword / in a large stone.
검이 있었다　　　　　　　　＿＿＿＿＿＿＿＿＿＿

2. These words were / on the stone: / "ONLY THE KING /
이런 글이 있었다　　　　돌 위에　　　　오직 왕만이

CAN TAKE THE SWORD / FROM THE STONE."
＿＿＿＿＿＿＿＿＿＿＿＿＿＿　돌에서

→ 〈pull A out of B〉는 'A를 당겨서 B에서 뽑다'라는 뜻이에요.

3. Every knight / tried to pull the sword / out of the stone.
모든 기사들은　　　＿＿＿＿＿＿＿＿＿＿＿＿　그 돌 밖으로

4. They pulled and pulled, / but nobody could pull it / out of the stone.
그들은 잡아당기고 또 잡아당겼다　　　＿＿＿＿＿＿＿＿＿＿＿＿＿＿　돌 밖으로

5. There was a big tournament / in the country.
＿＿＿＿＿＿＿＿＿＿＿＿＿　그 나라에서

→ knight에서 k는 발음되지 않아서 [nait]라고 발음해요.

6. Many knights came and fought / on horses / with swords in their hands.
많은 기사들이 와서 싸웠다　　　　말 위에서　　　＿＿＿＿＿＿＿＿＿＿＿＿＿＿

7. Arthur, a 15-year-old boy, / wanted to fight / with the other knights,
열다섯 살 소년인 아더는　　　　싸우고 싶었다　　　＿＿＿＿＿＿＿＿＿＿＿＿

/ too.
~도

8. But / he didn't have a sword.
하지만　　＿＿＿＿＿＿＿＿＿＿＿

9. Arthur went / to the stone.
아더는 갔다　　　　＿＿＿＿＿＿＿＿

44

10. He took the sword / in his hand / and pulled.

그는 검을 쥐었다 _______________ 그리고 잡아당겼다

11. It came out of the stone / easily.

_______________ 쉽게

12. There was a crowd / gathered around Arthur.

군중이 있었다 _______________

13. The crowd cheered, / and Arthur was crowned / King of England.

그 군중은 환호했다 _______________ 영국의 왕으로

crown은 '왕관'이라는 명사 외에 '왕위에 앉히다'라는 동사로도 쓰여요.
여기서는 수동태로 쓰인 거예요.

알아두면 문장이 쉽게
이해되는 그래머 포인트

Grammar Point   **nobody**

본문 쏙 **Nobody** could pull it out of the stone.
아무도 돌에서 그것을 빼낼 수 없었다.

nobody는 '아무도 ~않다'라는 뜻이에요. nobody 안에 '~않다'라는 뜻이 담겨 있으므로 따로 not을
쓰지 않는다는 점을 알아두세요. 동일한 뜻을 가진 단어로는 no one이 있어요. 만약에 사람이 아니라
사물이 '아무것도 ~않다'라고 하려면 nothing을 쓰면 됩니다.

확인문제 **1** Nobody knows what will happen next.

____

2 Nothing can stop us.

____

Rover

Mars

Rovers on Mars

Can people live on Mars? Maybe someday. Rovers are robots developed by NASA. These robots explore the surface of Mars and collect scientific data. Rovers help us learn about Mars. They are like robot scientists.

Rovers study rocks and soil to find signs of ancient life. They also check the weather on Mars. This is important for future trips where people might go to Mars. Rovers help us learn if Mars is safe for humans. They also search for useful things like water. They help scientists make safe homes and tools for people. Knowing more about Mars makes it easier for people to live there.

Thanks to rovers, the dream of living on Mars could come true one day!

- **develop** 개발하다
- **explore** 탐험하다
- **surface** 표면
- **collect** 모으다
- **scientific** 과학적인
- **sign** 신호, 징후
- **ancient** 고대의
- **life** 생명체
- **might** ~할지도 모른다
- **human** 인간
- **search** 찾다, 살펴보다
- **useful** 유용한
- **tool** 도구

Comprehension Check

A 문장을 읽고 옳으면 T(True), 틀리면 F(False)에 동그라미 하세요.

1 Rovers are developed by ancient people.   **T / F**

2 Rovers can check the weather on Mars.   **T / F**

3 Rovers are important for future trips.   **T / F**

B 다음을 읽고 알맞은 답을 고르세요.

1 This passage is mainly about ________________.

   ⓐ how helpful NASA is to us

   ⓑ how NASA's rovers help us understand Mars

   ⓒ how enjoyable traveling to Mars is

2 What do the rovers study on Mars to find signs of ancient life?

   ⓐ They study rocks and soil to find signs of ancient life.

   ⓑ They study robots to find signs of ancient life.

   ⓒ They study humans to find signs of ancient life.

3 Why is it important for rovers to find useful things like water on Mars?

   ⓐ Because it helps scientists find rocks.

   ⓑ Because it helps scientists build dams.

   ⓒ Because it helps scientists create safe homes and tools for people.

C 문장을 완성하는 단어를 써 넣으세요.

1 Rovers explore the __________ of Mars and collect __________ data.

2 This is important for future __________ where people might go to Mars.

3 Knowing more about __________ makes it easier for people to __________ there.

Read and Understand

● 잘 읽고 이해했나요? 문장의 정확한 의미를 알아보세요.

1. Can people live / on Mars? / Maybe / someday.
________________ 화성에서 ________ 아마도 ________

→ rover의 원래 의미인 '방랑자'에서 확장되어 여기서는 '탐사 로봇'을 뜻해요.

2. Rovers are robots / developed by NASA. NASA는 National Aeronautics and Space Administration의
로버는 로봇이다 ________________ → 줄임말로, '미국 항공 우주국'이라는 뜻이에요.

3. These robots explore / the surface of Mars / and collect /
이 로봇들은 탐사한다 ________________ 그리고 수집한다

scientific data.
____

4. Rovers help us / learn / about Mars.
________________ 알도록 화성에 대해

→ They는 앞에서 언급한 rovers를 말해요.

5. They are / like robot scientists.
그들은 ~이다 ________________

→ to find는 목적을 나타내는 부정사예요.

6. Rovers study / rocks and soil / to find signs of ancient life.
로버들은 연구한다 암석과 토양을 ________________

7. They also check / the weather / on Mars.
________________ 날씨를 화성에서

→ This는 앞에서 언급한 check the weather를 말해요. → where 이하는 어떤 future trips인지를 구체적으로 설명해 줘요.

8. This is important / for future trips / where people might go to Mars.
이것은 중요하다 ________________ 사람들이 화성에 갈지도 모르는

→ if는 '~인지 아닌지'로 해석해요.

9. Rovers help us / learn / if Mars is safe / for humans.
로버들은 우리를 도와준다 알도록 ________________ 인간에게

10. They also search for / useful things / like water.
그들은 또한 찾는다 ________________ 물 같은

11. They help scientists / make / safe homes and tools for people.
그들은 과학자들을 돕는다　　　　만들도록

12. Knowing more about Mars / makes it easier / for people /
　　　　　　　　　　　　　더 쉽게 만들어준다　　　사람들에게

to live there.
그곳에서 사는 것을

13. Thanks to rovers, / the dream of living on Mars / could come true /
로버들 덕분에　　　　　　　　　　　　　　　　　　　실현될 수 있다

one day!
언젠가

Grammar Point　동명사 knowing

본문 쏙　Knowing more about Mars makes it easier for people to live there.

화성에 대해 더 많이 아는 것은 사람들이 그곳에서 사는 것을 더 쉽게 만듭니다.

동명사는 동사에 –ing를 붙여 만든 단어로, 명사처럼 쓰이지만 동작이나 상태를 설명할 수 있어요. 여기서는 knowing(아는 것)이 명사로 쓰여 makes it easier라는 서술어의 주어가 돼요. 여기서 it은 to live there(그곳에서 사는 것을)를 가리키는 가목적어로, '그것'이라고 해석하지 않아요.

확인문제　**1**　Exercising regularly makes it easier to stay healthy.

2　Learning a new language makes it easier for travelers to communicate.

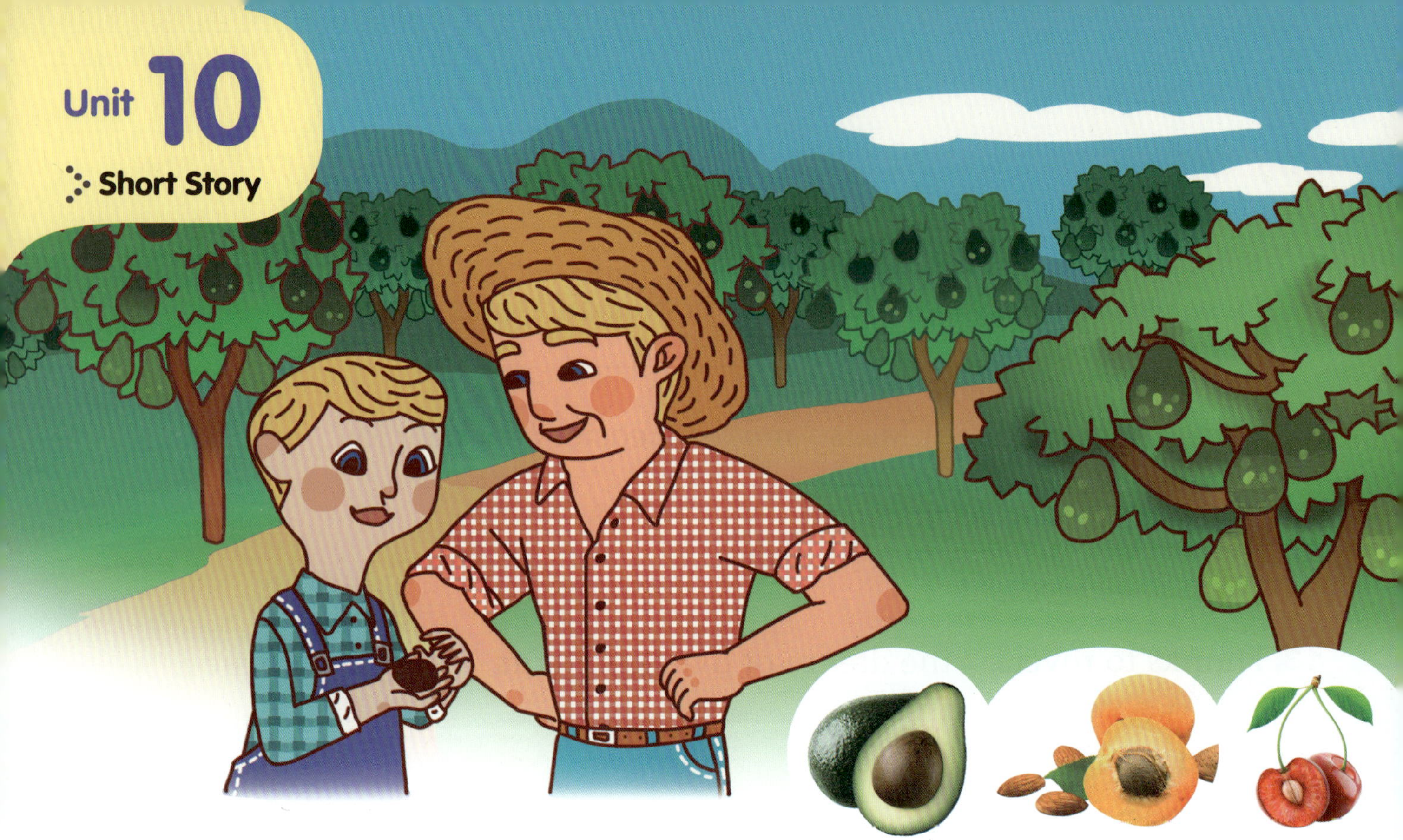

My Uncle's Orchard

Jerry visited his uncle's orchard. There were a lot of different kinds of fruit trees. He also found many fruit seeds on the ground. They all had different sizes, shapes, and colors.

Jerry wondered what kind of seeds they were, so he asked his uncle. He picked up a seed which was as big as a ping-pong ball. It was brown and round. His uncle said that it was an avocado seed. Then Jerry held a flat and oval-shaped seed that was the size of a coin. That was an apricot seed.

He found a seed that he knew. It was the seed of his favorite fruit. It looked like a pea and it was beige. Yes! It was a cherry seed.

- **uncle** 삼촌
- **orchard** 과수원
- **kind** 종류
- **seed** 씨앗
- **wonder** 궁금해하다
- **pick up** 집어 들다
- **ping-pong ball** 탁구공
- **avocado** 아보카도
- **held** (손에) 들었다 (hold (손에) 들다)
- **flat** 납작한
- **oval** 타원형
- **coin** 동전
- **apricot** 살구
- **pea** 완두콩
- **beige** 베이지색

Comprehension Check

A 문장을 읽고 옳으면 T(True), 틀리면 F(False)에 동그라미 하세요.

1 There were a lot of different kinds of fruit trees in the orchard.　**T / F**

2 Jerry's favorite fruit is apricot.　**T / F**

3 An avocado seed is as big as a ping-pong ball.　**T / F**

B 다음을 읽고 알맞은 답을 고르세요.

1 This passage is mainly about _______________.

ⓐ uncle's house

ⓑ fruit trees

ⓒ fruit seeds

2 What is Jerry's favorite fruit?

ⓐ Avocado

ⓑ Apricot

ⓒ Cherry

3 What does an apricot seed look like?

ⓐ It's very big and it's brown and round.

ⓑ It's flat and oval-shaped and it's the size of a coin.

ⓒ It looks like a pea and it is beige.

C 문장을 완성하는 단어를 써 넣으세요.

1 There were a lot of different ___________ of fruit trees.

2 Jerry found many fruit seeds on the ___________.

3 He picked up a seed which was as ___________ as a ping-pong ball.

● 잘 읽고 이해했나요? 문장의 정확한 의미를 알아보세요.

1. Jerry visited / his uncle's orchard.
제리는 방문했다 _______________________

→ 여기에서 kind는 '친절한'이 아니라 '종류'를 뜻해요.

2. There were / a lot of different kinds / of fruit trees.
있었다 _______________________ 과일 나무들의

found는 find의 과거형이에요.

3. He also found / many fruit seeds / on the ground.
그는 또한 발견했다 _______________________ 땅에서

4. They all had / different sizes, shapes, and colors.
그들은 모두 갖고 있었다 _______________________

5. Jerry wondered / what kind of seeds they were, / so he asked his uncle.
제리는 궁금했다 _______________________ 그래서 그는 그의 삼촌에게 물어봤다

→ as big as는 '~만큼 큰'이라고 해석해요.

6. He picked up / a seed / which was as big as a ping-pong ball.
그는 집어 들었다   씨앗 한 개를 _______________________

7. It was / brown and round.
그것은 ~였다 _______________________

8. His uncle said / that it was an avocado seed.
그의 삼촌은 말했다 _______________________

that ~ coin이 seed를 꾸며주고 있어요.

9. Then Jerry held / a flat and oval-shaped seed / that was the size of a
그 다음에 제리는 들었다   납작하고 타원형인 씨앗을 _______________________

coin.
____

10. That was / an apricot seed.
그것은 ~였다 _______________________

11. He found / a seed / that he knew.

그는 찾았다　　　씨앗 한 개를 ________________

12. It was the seed / of his favorite fruit.

그것은 씨앗이었다 ____________________

13. It looked like a pea / and it was beige.　Yes!　It was a cherry seed.

________________________ 그리고 그것은 베이지색이었다　맞아　그것은 체리 씨였다.

Grammar Point　　**명사(사물)를 뒤에서 꾸며주는 which절**

본문 쏙　He picked up a seed **which** was as big as a ping-pong ball.

그는 탁구공만큼 큰 씨앗 하나를 집었다.

여기서 which는 앞에 나온 명사 a seed에 대해 설명하기 위해 쓰였어요. 따라서 밑줄 친 which절이 a seed를 꾸며주는 것이므로 a seed ~ ball을 '탁구공만큼 큰 씨앗'이라고 해석하면 됩니다. 이런 용도로 쓰는 which를 '관계대명사'라고 하고, which 대신 that을 쓰기도 해요.

확인문제　**1**　I need a hat which goes well with this skirt.

　2　We found bread which was as big as a soccer ball.

Up 3 5형식 문장 해석하기 – 사역동사 let

| 무엇은 | | ~하게 한다 | 누가 | ~하도록 |

These fun facts / let / us / identify the animals easily.
이런 재미있는 사실들은   하게 했다 우리가   그 동물들을 쉽게 알아보도록

해설 이런 재미있는 사실들은 우리가 그 동물들을 쉽게 알아보게 해줬어요.

'주어+동사+목적어+목적보어'로 이루어진 5형식 문장이에요. 이런 구조의 문장에서 동사 let은 뒤에 목적어와 목적보어인 동사원형을 함께 써서 '~를 …하게 하다, …하게 허락하다'라는 뜻으로 해석해요. 목적보어 자리에 동사원형이 오기 때문에 identify 원형 그대로 썼어요. 이 문장에서는 '우리가 그 동물들을 쉽게 알아보게 했다'라고 해석해요.

A 문장을 슬래시(/)로 끊어 읽은 후 우리말 해석을 완성하세요.

1 The story let us explore a magical world quickly.

→ 그 이야기는 / 하게 했다 / 우리가 / ______________________________

2 Mom let my brother invite his friends for a pizza party.

→ 엄마는 / 하게 했다 / 내 남동생이 / ______________________________

3 My teacher let me remember the important lesson for the test.

→ 내 선생님은 / 하게 했다 / 내가 / ______________________________

B 우리말 문장과 일치하도록 영어문장을 알맞게 배열하세요.

1 그의 친구의 힌트는 그가 어려운 퍼즐을 빠르게 풀게 해주었다.

(let / his friend's hints / solve / him / the difficult puzzles faster)

→ ______________________________.

2 재미있는 실험들은 우리가 자연에 대해 새로운 것을 발견하게 해주었다.

(us / discover / let / the fun experiments / new things about nature)

→ ______________________________.

Up 4 관계대명사로 길어진 문장 해석하기 – which

누가　　　한다　　　　무엇을　　　　　어떤

He / **picked up** / **a seed** / **which was as big as a ping-pong ball.**
그는　　　　집었다　　　씨앗 하나를　　　　　　　　　탁구공만큼 큰

해설 그는 탁구공만큼 큰 씨앗 하나를 집었어요.

3형식(주어+동사+목적어) 문장 구조이며, 목적어를 수식하는 which 관계대명사절이 따라 붙은 형태예요. which 관계대명사절은 앞에 오는 명사 a seed를 수식하여 '탁구공만큼 큰' 씨앗이라는 의미를 만듭니다. 이 관계대명사절은 a seed가 어떤 씨앗인지 부연 설명하는 형용사 역할을 합니다.

A 문장을 슬래시(/)로 끊어 읽은 후 우리말 해석을 완성하세요.

1 She owns a cat which always follows her around.

→ 그녀는 / 키운다 / _________________ / 항상 그녀를 따라다니는

2 I saw a car which was painted in bright red.

→ 나는 / 보았다 / 차 한 대를 / _______________________

3 He told a story which made everyone laugh.

→ _______________ / _______________ / _______________ / 모두를 웃게 만든

B 우리말 문장과 일치하도록 영어문장을 알맞게 배열하세요.

1 그들은 나무로 둘러싸인 집에서 산다.

(which / in a house / they live / is surrounded / by trees)

→ ____.

2 그녀는 그녀를 매우 기쁘게 만든 편지를 받았다.

(made her very happy / which / a letter / she received)

→ ____.

Thanksgiving Day

Thanksgiving Day is celebrated on the fourth Thursday in November in the USA. It is celebrated as a day of harvesting crops.

In the winter of 1620, half of the English people known as Pilgrims starved to death because they had failed to harvest crops in the USA. Native Americans taught the Pilgrims how to grow and harvest crops. The next year, in 1621, the Pilgrims succeeded in harvesting crops.

The Pilgrims invited the Native Americans to celebrate the successful harvest. The Pilgrims and the Native Americans ate corn, beans, and pumpkins. They also caught fish and ate them together. This is why Americans celebrate Thanksgiving Day.

- **Thanksgiving Day** 추수감사절
- **celebrate** 기념하다
- **November** 11월
- **harvest** 수확하다; 수확
- **crop** 농작물
- **known as** ~로 알려진
- **Pilgrim** 청교도 (1620년에 메이플라워호를 타고 미국으로 간 영국인 이주민)
- **starve** 굶주리다
- **fail** 실패하다
- **native** 원주민의
- **American** 미국인
- **succeed** 성공하다
- **invite** 초대하다
- **successful** 성공적인
- **pumpkin** 호박

Comprehension Check

A 문장을 읽고 옳으면 T(True), 틀리면 F(False)에 동그라미 하세요.

1 In America, Thanksgiving Day is celebrated in November.   **T / F**

2 Thanksgiving Day is celebrated as a day of planting crops.   **T / F**

3 The Pilgrims taught the Native Americans how to grow crops.   **T / F**

B 다음을 읽고 알맞은 답을 고르세요.

1 This passage is mainly about _______________.

　ⓐ Thanksgiving Day

　ⓑ the Pilgrims

　ⓒ harvesting the crops

2 Why did many Pilgrims starve to death?

　ⓐ Because Native Americans caught fish and ate them.

　ⓑ Because they had failed to harvest crops in the USA.

　ⓒ Because Native Americans taught them how to grow and harvest crops.

3 Why did the Pilgrims invite the Native Americans to a feast?

　ⓐ To celebrate the successful harvest

　ⓑ To travel to England together

　ⓒ To grow and harvest crops

C 문장을 완성하는 단어를 써 넣으세요.

1 Thanksgiving Day is celebrated on the __________ Thursday in __________ in the USA.

2 The next year, in 1621, the Pilgrims __________ in harvesting crops.

3 The Pilgrims and the Native Americans ate corn, beans, and __________.

Read and Understand

● 잘 읽고 이해했나요? 문장의 정확한 의미를 알아보세요.

1. Thanksgiving Day / is celebrated / on the fourth Thursday /
추수감사절은 　　　　　　기념된다

→ 요일 앞에는 전치사 on을 넣어요.

in November / in the USA.
11월의　　　　　　미국에서

→ is celebrated는 수동태로서 '기념된다'라는 뜻이에요.

2. It is celebrated / as a day of harvesting crops.
그것은 기념된다

→ half of는 '~의 절반'이라는 뜻이에요.

3. In the winter of 1620, / half of the English people / known as Pilgrims /
1620년 겨울에　　　　　　영국 사람들의 절반이　　　　　　청교도로 알려진

→ starve to death는 '굶어 죽다'라는 의미예요.

starved to death / because they had failed / to harvest crops /
　　　　　　　　그들이 실패했기 때문에　　　　　　농작물을 수확하는 것을

in the USA.
미국에서

4. Native Americans taught / the Pilgrims / how to grow and harvest
미국 원주민들은 가르쳐 줬다　　　　그 청교도들에게

crops.

→ succeed in은 '~에 성공하다'라는 뜻이에요.

5. The next year, in 1621, / the Pilgrims succeeded / in harvesting crops.
그 다음 해인　　　　1621년에　　　　　　　　　　농작물을 수확하는 것에

6. The Pilgrims invited / the Native Americans / to celebrate /
청교도들은 초대했다　　　　미국 원주민들을　　　　　　기념하기 위해

the successful harvest.

7. The Pilgrims and the Native Americans ate / corn, beans, and pumpkins.

청교도들과 미국 원주민들은 먹었다

8. They also / caught fish / and ate them together.

그들은 또한   물고기를 잡았다

9. This is why / Americans celebrate / Thanksgiving Day.

__________   미국인들은 기념한다   추수감사절을

Grammar Point   had+과거분사

본문 쏙 Half of the English people known as Pilgrims <u>starved</u> to death because they had failed to harvest crops in the USA.

청교도로 알려진 영국 사람들의 절반이 미국에서 농작물을 수확하는 데 실패해서 굶어 죽었다.

because를 이용해 두 절(주어+동사)을 연결한 형태예요. 그런데 앞에 나온 절에는 과거형인 starved 를 썼는데, 왜 뒤에 나온 절에는 had failed를 썼을까요? 그것은 청교도인들이 굶어 죽은 것보다 추수 에 실패한 것이 먼저 일어난 일이기 때문이에요. 이렇게 과거보다 더 이전에 일어난 일을 나타낼 때는 〈had+과거분사〉 형태를 사용하는데, 이를 '과거 완료'라고 해요.

확인문제   **1** They had finished their lunch when I arrived.

2 She had lived in this house before I moved here.

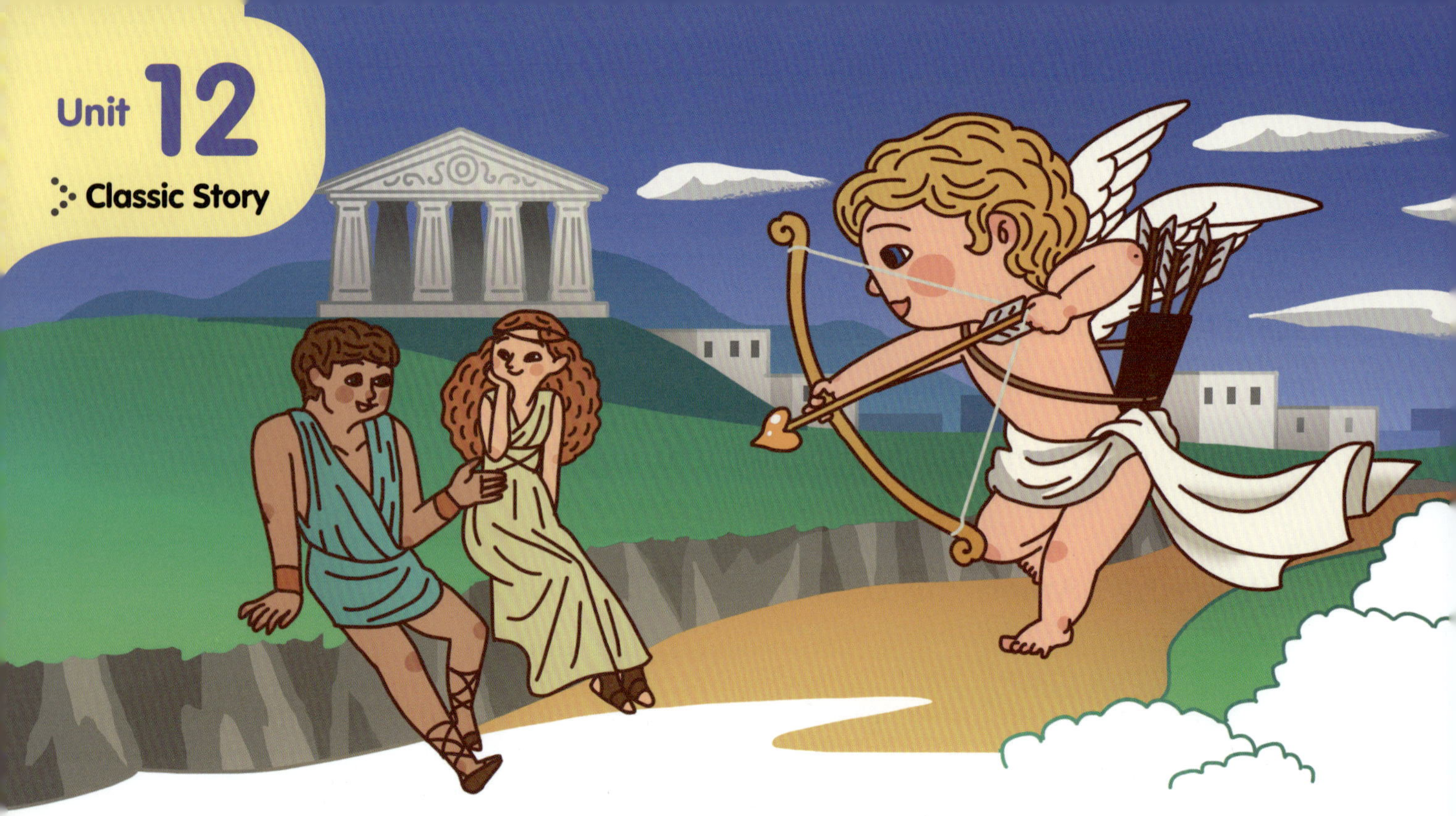

Cupid

Cupid was the Roman god of love. He was also called Eros in Greek. He was the son of Venus, the goddess of love and beauty.

There were myths about Cupid and his arrows. Cupid's arrows could make you fall in love. Cupid had wings on his back, so he could fly. He carried a bow and two types of arrows. One had a sharp golden point, and the other had a blunt lead point.

When Cupid shot a person with the golden arrow, this person fell in love with the very next person he or she saw. But when Cupid shot someone with the lead arrow, this person hated the next person he or she saw.

So watch out! Cupid might shoot you someday.

- **Roman** 로마의
- **god** 신
- **Greek** 그리스어
- **goddess** 여신
- **beauty** 아름다움
- **myth** 신화
- **arrow** 화살
- **bow** 활
- **point** (사물의 뾰족한) 끝
- **blunt** 뭉툭한
- **lead** 납
- **shot** 쐈다
- **shoot** 쏘다
- **someone** 누군가
- **watch out** 조심하다

Comprehension Check

A 문장을 읽고 옳으면 T(True), 틀리면 F(False)에 동그라미 하세요.

1 Venus was the Roman god of love.　　　　　　　　**T / F**

2 Cupid carried a bow and two types of arrows.　　　**T / F**

3 When Cupid shot a person with the lead arrow, this
person fell in love with someone.　　　　　　　　**T / F**

B 다음을 읽고 알맞은 답을 고르세요.

1 This passage is mainly about ________________.

　ⓐ Roman　　　　　ⓑ Cupid's arrows　　　　　ⓒ Falling in love

2 Which arrows made a person hate the next person he or she saw?

　ⓐ The golden arrows

　ⓑ The green arrows

　ⓒ The lead arrows

3 According to the story, what is true about Cupid?

　ⓐ Cupid stole his arrows from Zeus.

　ⓑ Cupid had wings on his back.

　ⓒ Venus was the son of Cupid.

C 문장을 완성하는 단어를 써 넣으세요.

1 Cupid was also called __________ in Greek.

2 When Cupid shot a person with the __________ arrow, this person fell in
__________ with the very next person he or she saw.

3 So watch __________! Cupid might __________ you someday.

● 잘 읽고 이해했나요? 문장의 정확한 의미를 알아보세요.

1. Cupid was / the Roman god / of love.
　　큐피드는 ~였다　　　　　　　　　　　　　　　사랑의

2. He was also called / Eros / in Greek.
　　그는 또한 불렸다　　　　　에로스라고

'~ 언어로'라고 할 때는 in을 넣어서
in Greek(그리스어로), in English(영어로)라고 표현해요.

3. He was the son of Venus, / the goddess of love and beauty.
　　그는 비너스의 아들이었다

4. There were myths / about Cupid and his arrows.
　　　　　　　　　　　　큐피드와 그의 화살에 관한

⟨make A B⟩는 'A를 B하게 만들다'라는 표현이고,
fall in love는 '사랑에 빠지다'라는 뜻이에요.

5. Cupid's arrows / could make / you / fall in love.
　　큐피드의 화살은　　　　만들 수 있다　　당신을

6. Cupid had wings / on his back, / so he could fly.
　　큐피드는 날개를 갖고 있었다　　　　　　그래서 그는 날 수 있었다

7. He carried / a bow and two types of arrows.
　　그는 가지고 다녔다

point를 꾸며주는 형용사 두 개가 나란히 온 구조예요.

8. One had / a sharp golden point, / and the other had /
　　하나는 갖고 있었다　날카로운 금 화살촉을　　　　그리고 다른 하나는 갖고 있었다

a blunt lead point.

9. When Cupid shot a person / with the golden arrow, /
　　큐피드가 사람을 쏘면　　　　　　　　　　금 화살로

he or she는 남자인지
여자인지 모르는 상황에서
사용해요.

여기에서 very는 '바로 그'라는 뜻으로 쓰였어요.

this person fell in love / with the very next person / he or she saw.
이 사람은 사랑에 빠졌다　　　　　　　　　　　　　　　　　그나 그녀가 본

10. But / when Cupid shot someone / with the lead arrow, /

그러나 　　　　　　　　　　　　　　　　　　納 화살로

this person hated / the next person / he or she saw.

이 사람은 미워했다　　　　다음 사람을　　　　그나 그녀가 본

might는 '~일지도 모른다'는 뜻의 조동사예요.

11. So watch out!　Cupid might shoot you / someday.

그러니 조심해라 　　　　　　　　　　　　　　　언젠가

Grammar Point　one과 the other

본문 쏙 One had a sharp golden point, and the other had a blunt lead point.

한 종류는 날카로운 금 화살촉이 있었고, 다른 한 종류는 뭉툭한 납 화살촉이 있었어요.

두 가지의 사물을 두고 하나씩 설명하는 경우가 있지요. 이럴 경우 첫 번째 것을 설명할 때는 one(하나)을 사용하고, 두 번째 것을 설명할 때는 the other(다른 하나)를 사용해요. 세 가지의 사물을 하나씩 설명할 때는 one(하나), another(또 하나), the other(나머지 하나)의 순서로 사용하면 돼요.

확인문제 **1** One is black, and the other is blue.

2 One cup has milk, and the other has juice.

Unit 13

Nonfiction

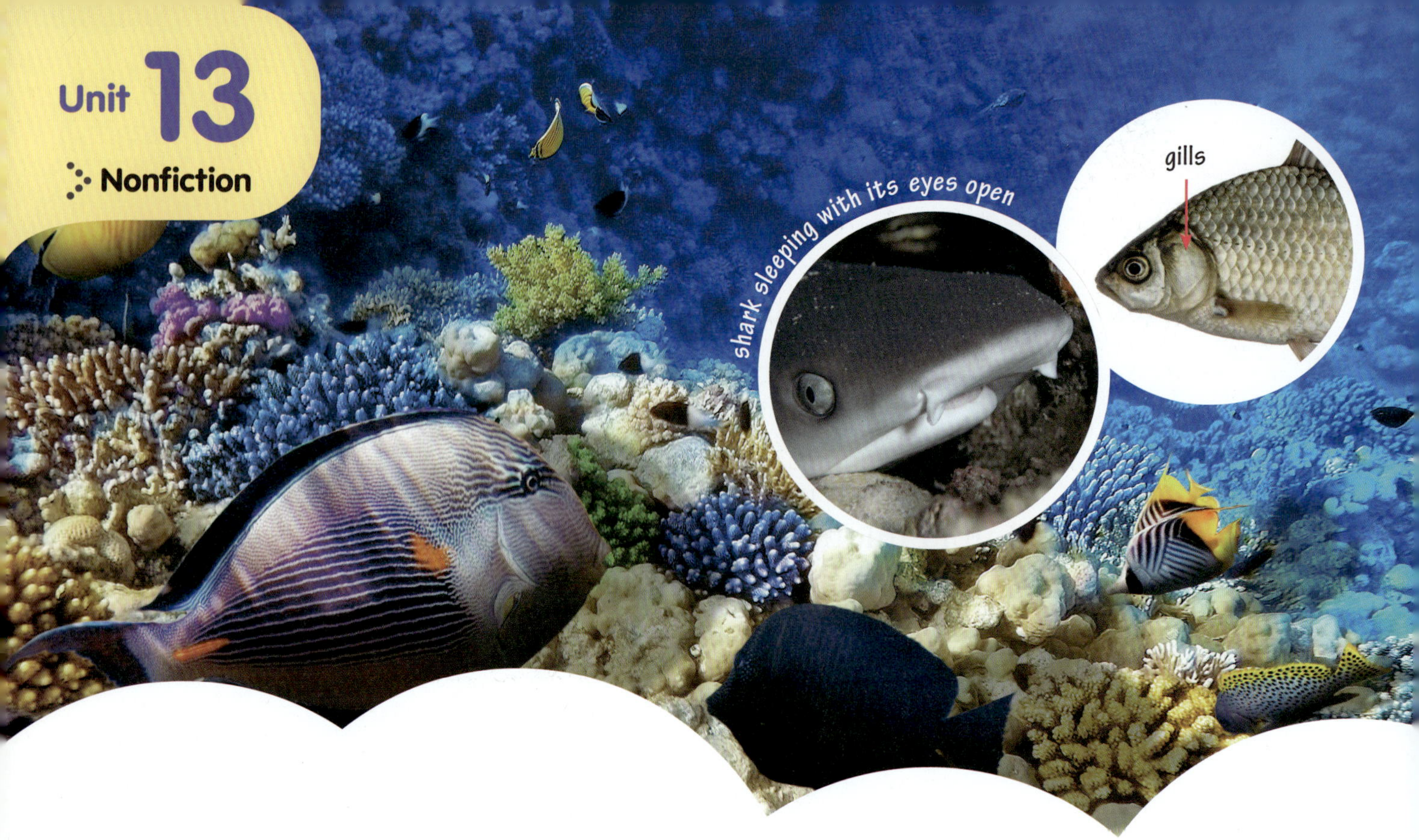

All About Fish

Fish spend their entire lives in water. There are 32,000 different species of fish. Some fish are up to 2,700 centimeters long and others are only 8 millimeters long.

Fish need oxygen to live, just like humans. Humans have lungs to breathe air, but fish have gills. Gills help fish breathe under water.

Like humans, fish also sleep. They sleep with their eyes open because they don't have eyelids. But there are always exceptions. Some sharks have eyelids. But they sleep with their eyes open. If you see a fish moving slowly, it might be sleeping. Most fish move when they're sleeping because they need to breathe oxygen.

- **spend** (시간을) 보내다
- **entire** 전체의
- **lives** 삶들 (life 삶)
- **species** (생물) 종
- **oxygen** 산소
- **human** 인간, 사람
- **lung** 허파
- **breathe** 호흡하다
- **gill** 아가미
- **eyelid** 눈꺼풀
- **always** 항상
- **exception** 예외
- **shark** 상어

Comprehension Check

A 문장을 읽고 옳으면 T(True), 틀리면 F(False)에 동그라미 하세요.

1 Fish spend their entire lives in water.   **T / F**

2 There are many different species of fish.   **T / F**

3 Fish have lungs to breathe air like humans.   **T / F**

B 다음을 읽고 알맞은 답을 고르세요.

1 This passage is mainly about ______________.

   ⓐ water   **ⓑ** fish   **ⓒ** gills

2 Why do fish sleep with their eyes open?

   ⓐ Because fish don't have lungs.

   ⓑ Because fish don't have eyelids.

   ⓒ Because fish don't have brains.

3 How can fish breathe under the water?

   ⓐ Fish breathe through their lungs.

   ⓑ Fish breathe through their eyelids.

   ⓒ Fish breathe through their gills.

C 문장을 완성하는 단어를 써 넣으세요.

1 ___________ help fish breathe under water.

2 Some ___________ have eyelids.

3 If you see a fish moving slowly, it might be ___________.

Read and Understand

● 잘 읽고 이해했나요? 문장의 정확한 의미를 알아보세요.

→ entire life는 '평생'이라는 뜻이에요.

1. Fish spend / their entire lives / in water.
물고기는 보낸다 _______________ 물속에서

2. There are / 32,000 different species / of fish.
있다 _______________ 물고기의

→ some은 어떤 무리 중에 '일부'를 나타내고, others는 그 무리 중 '다른 일부'를 나타내요.

3. Some fish are / up to 2,700 centimeters long / and others are /
어떤 물고기는 ~이다 _______________ 또 어떤 물고기는 ~이다

only 8 millimeters long.
길이가 8mm밖에

4. Fish need oxygen / to live, / just like humans.
물고기는 산소가 필요하다 _______________ 사람처럼

→ breath는 '호흡'이라는 명사이고, breathe는 '호흡하다'라는 동사예요.

5. Humans have lungs / to breathe air, / but fish have gills.
사람들은 허파를 가지고 있다 _______________ 하지만 물고기들은 아가미를 가지고 있다

6. Gills help / fish breathe / under water.
아가미는 도와준다   물고기들이 호흡하도록 _______________

7. Like humans, / fish also sleep.
_______________ 물고기도 잠을 잔다

8. They sleep / with their eyes open / because / they don't have / eyelids.
그들은 잠을 잔다 _______________ 왜냐하면   그들은 갖고 있지 않다   눈꺼풀을

9. But / there are / always exceptions.
하지만   있다 _______________

10. Some sharks / have eyelids.   But they sleep / with their eyes open.
어떤 상어들은 _______________ 하지만 그들은 잔다   눈을 뜬 채로

11. If you see a fish / moving slowly, / it might be sleeping.

당신이 물고기를 보면　　　천천히 움직이는

12. Most fish move / when they're sleeping / because / they need /

대부분의 물고기는 움직인다　　　　　　　　왜냐하면　　　그들은 필요하다

to breathe oxygen.

산소를 호흡하는 것이

Grammar Point 　태도·방식을 나타내는 **with**

본문 쏙 They sleep <u>with</u> their eyes open.

그들은 눈을 뜬 채 잠을 잔다.

with는 '~와 함께'라는 뜻뿐만 아니라 '~한 채'라는 뜻도 갖고 있어요. 즉, 어떤 일을 할 때의 태도나 방식 등을 나타낼 때 with를 사용할 수 있답니다. 따라서 위 문장에서 with their eyes open은 '그들의 눈을 뜬 채'라고 해석하면 됩니다.

확인문제 　**1** He walks with his hands in his pockets.

2 She laughs with her mouth covered.

Jenny's Closet

Jenny had a big messy closet in her room. She liked to put all her stuff in the closet. She put her clothes, caps, socks, bags, dolls, hair pins, and even shoes in it. Her mother always told her to clean out the closet. But Jenny liked it that way.

One day, Jenny was invited to a friend's birthday party. She wanted to wear her purple shirt, but she couldn't find it. Jenny bent over and finally found a piece of the shirt at the back of the closet. She pulled it hard. Suddenly, everything came out with the shirt. Jenny was buried under her stuff, and her purple shirt was ripped.

"From now on, I'll never have a messy closet again."

- **messy** 지저분한
- **closet** 옷장
- **stuff** 물건
- **even**
  (심지어) ~까지[조차]
- **bent** 굽혔다
  (bend 굽히다)
- **finally** 마침내
- **piece** 일부, 부품
- **back** 뒤쪽
- **bury**
  (보이지 않게) 묻다
- **rip** 찢다
- **from now on**
  앞으로는
- **never** 절대 ~않다

68

Comprehension Check

A 문장을 읽고 옳으면 T(True), 틀리면 F(False)에 동그라미 하세요.

1 Jenny liked to put all her stuff in the closet. **T / F**

2 Jenny always told her mom to clean out the closet. **T / F**

3 Jenny's purple shirt was not in the closet. **T / F**

B 다음을 읽고 알맞은 답을 고르세요.

1 This passage is mainly about ________________.

   a a purple shirt

   b Jenny and her mother

   c a messy closet

2 Why did Jenny want to wear her purple shirt?

   a Because she was invited to a friend's birthday party.

   b Because she had to go to school.

   c Because she wanted to visit her grandparents.

3 What happened to Jenny's purple shirt?

   a It was cleaned in the washing machine.

   b It was ripped.

   c It was not in the closet.

C 문장을 완성하는 단어를 써 넣으세요.

1 She put her clothes, caps, socks, bags, dolls, hair pins, and __________ shoes in it.

2 Jenny was _________ under her stuff, and her purple shirt was _________.

3 From now on, I'll __________ have a messy closet again.

Read and Understand

● 잘 읽고 이해했나요? 문장의 정확한 의미를 알아보세요.

1. Jenny had / a big messy closet / in her room.

제니는 갖고 있었다 ___________________ 자신의 방에

→ stuff는 물건의 이름을 모르거나 이름이 중요하지 않을 때 쓰는 단어예요.

2. She liked to put / all her stuff / in the closet.

그녀는 넣는 것을 좋아했다 _____________ 그 옷장 안에

3. She put / her clothes, caps, socks, bags, dolls, hair pins, /

그녀는 넣었다　그녀의 옷들, 모자들, 양말들, 가방들, 인형들, 머리핀들,

and even shoes / in it.

___________________ 그 안에

→ clean out은 '깨끗이 치우다'라는 뜻이에요.

4. Her mother always / told her / to clean out the closet.

그녀의 어머니는 항상　　그녀에게 말했다 ___________________

→ that way는 '그런 방식으로, 그런 상태로'라고 해석해요.

5. But Jenny liked it / that way.

그러나 제니는 그것을 좋아했다 __________

→ was invited는 수동태이므로 '초대받았다'는 뜻이에요.

6. One day, / Jenny was invited / to a friend's birthday party.

어느 날 ___________________ 친구의 생일 파티에

7. She wanted to wear / her purple shirt, / but she couldn't find it.

그녀는 입고 싶었다 ___________________ 하지만 그녀는 그것을 찾을 수가 없었다

→ bend over는 '허리를[몸을] 구부리다'라는 뜻이에요.

8. Jenny bent over / and finally found / a piece of the shirt /

제니는 허리를 구부렸다 ___________________ 그 셔츠의 일부를

at the back of the closet.

옷장의 뒤쪽에서

→ 여기서 hard는 '힘껏, 세게'라는 뜻의 부사로 쓰였어요.

9. She / pulled it hard.

그녀는 ___________________

10. Suddenly, / everything came out / with the shirt.

갑자기 ___________________ 그 셔츠와 함께

70

11. Jenny was buried / under her stuff, / and her purple shirt / was ripped.

제니는 묻혔다   그녀의 물건들 아래에   그리고 그녀의 보라색 셔츠는

12. "From now on, / I'll never have / a messy closet / again."

나는 절대 갖지 않을 것이다   지저분한 옷장을   다시는

Grammar Point | **tell A to B**

본문 쏙 Her mother always told her to clean out the closet.

그녀의 어머니는 항상 그녀에게 옷장을 깨끗이 치우라고 말했다.

〈tell A(목적어) to B(동사)〉는 'A에게 B하라고 말하다'라는 뜻이에요. 따라서 told her to clean up 은 '그녀에게 깨끗이 치우라고 말했다'라고 해석하면 됩니다.

확인문제 **1** The doctor told me to rest in bed.

2 I told him to call me today.

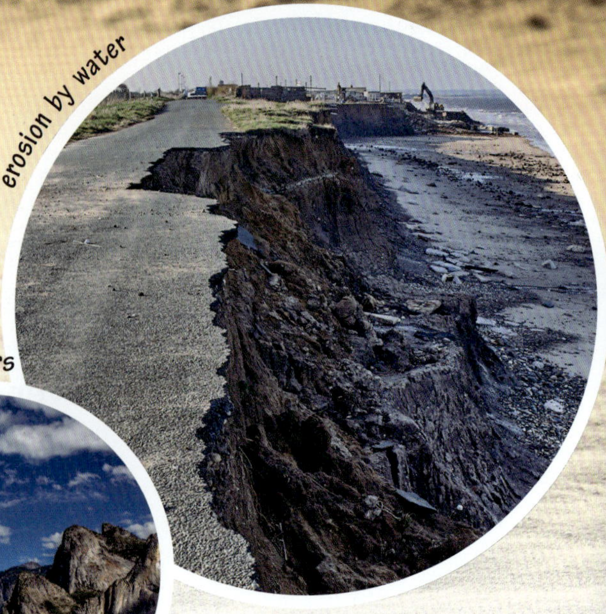

Water, Wind, and Ice

Water, wind, and ice wear away the land. This is called erosion. Erosion is the removal of rocks and soil by wind, water, ice, and gravity. Erosion changes the earth's surface. This can change mountain peaks, valleys, and coastlines. Erosion can happen quickly or take thousands of years.

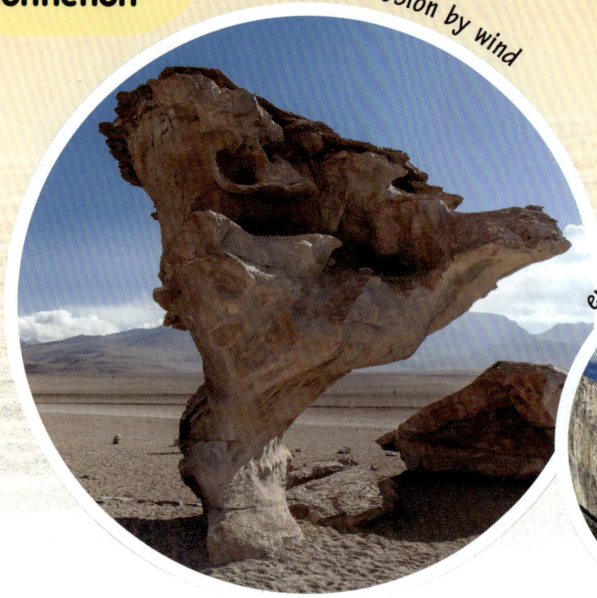

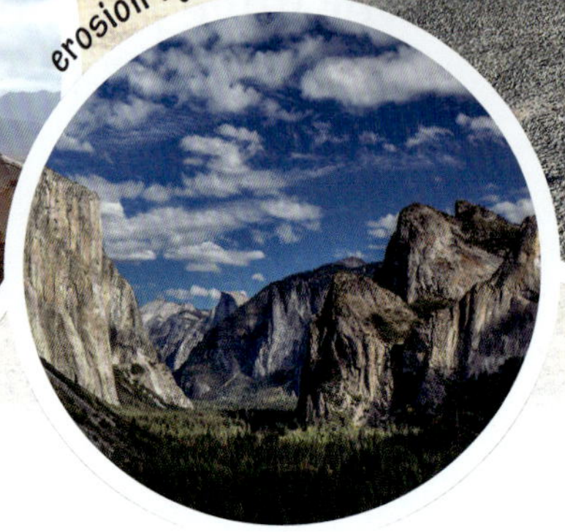

Do you know why streams and lakes get muddy after a rainstorm? It is a sign that erosion is taking place. Rainstorms change the landscape.

Wind causes erosion, especially in dry areas. Wind picks up and carries away sand, light rocks, and pebbles. Wind changes the landscape, too. Ice causes erosion in cold areas. Giant rivers of ice, called glaciers, move slowly and change the valleys and mountains.

- **wear away** 닳아 없애다
- **erosion** 침식
- **removal** 제거
- **gravity** 중력
- **surface** 표면
- **peak** 산꼭대기
- **valley** 계곡
- **coastline** 해안선
- **stream** 개울, 냇물
- **muddy** 진흙투성이인
- **rainstorm** 폭풍우
- **take place** 발생하다
- **landscape** 풍경
- **area** 지역
- **carry away** 휩쓸어 가다
- **pebble** 자갈
- **glacier** 빙하

Comprehension Check

A 문장을 읽고 옳으면 T(True), 틀리면 F(False)에 동그라미 하세요.

1 Erosion changes the Earth's surface.　　　　　　　　**T / F**

2 Erosion always happens quickly.　　　　　　　　　　**T / F**

3 Wind causes erosion, especially in cold areas.　　　**T / F**

B 다음을 읽고 알맞은 답을 고르세요.

1 This passage is mainly about _______________.

　ⓐ gravity

　ⓑ the earth's surface

　ⓒ erosion

2 What does NOT cause erosion?

　ⓐ Landscape

　ⓑ Ice

　ⓒ Gravity

3 What are giant rivers of ice called?

　ⓐ Streams

　ⓑ Glaciers

　ⓒ Coastlines

C 문장을 완성하는 단어를 써 넣으세요.

1 Water, wind, and ice __________ away the land.

2 Erosions can __________ mountain __________, valleys, and coastlines.

3 Erosion can happen quickly or take __________ of years.

Read and Understand

● 잘 읽고 이해했나요? 문장의 정확한 의미를 알아보세요.

→ wear(닳다)에 away가 붙으면 '닳아 없애다'라는 뜻이 돼요.

1. Water, wind, and ice / wear away the land.   This is called / erosion.
물, 바람, 그리고 얼음은 _______________ 이것은 불린다   침식이라고

→ 여기에서 by는 '~에 의해'라는 뜻이에요.

2. Erosion is / the removal of rocks and soil / by wind, water, ice, and
침식은 ~이다 _______________ 바람, 물, 얼음, 그리고 중력에 의해

gravity.

3. Erosion changes / the Earth's surface.
침식은 변화시킨다 _______________

→ this는 앞에서 언급한 '침식'을 말해요.

4. This can change / mountain peaks, valleys, and coastlines.
_______________ 산꼭대기, 계곡, 그리고 해안선을

→ take 뒤에 시간이 나오면 take는 '(시간이) 걸리다'라는 의미예요.

5. Erosion can happen / quickly / or take thousands of years.
침식은 일어날 수 있다   빠르게 _______________

6. Do you know / why streams and lakes get muddy / after a rainstorm?
당신은 알고 있는가? _______________ 폭풍우가 온 뒤에

7. It is a sign / that erosion is taking place.
그것은 표시이다 _______________

8. Rainstorms change / the landscape.
폭풍우는 변화시킨다 _______________

9. Wind causes / erosion, / especially in dry areas.
바람은 일으킨다   침식을 _______________

→ carry away는 '~을 가져가 버리다, 휩쓸어 가다'라는 뜻이에요.

10. Wind picks up / and carries away / sand, light rocks, and pebbles.
바람은 들어 올린다 _______________ 모래, 가벼운 암석들, 그리고 자갈들을

11. Wind changes / the landscape, too.
_______________ 풍경도

74

12. Ice causes / erosion / in cold areas.

얼음은 일으킨다　　침식을　　＿＿＿＿＿＿＿＿＿＿

13. Giant rivers of ice, / called glaciers, / move slowly / and change /

거대한 얼음 강들이　　＿＿＿＿＿＿＿＿＿＿　　천천히 움직인다　　그리고 변화시킨다

the valleys and mountains.

계곡들과 산들을

Grammar Point　get + 형용사

본문 쏙 Do you know why streams and lakes get muddy after a rainstorm?

폭풍우가 온 뒤에 계곡과 호수가 왜 진흙탕이 되는지 알고 있나요?

동사 get은 '~해지다, ~하게 되다'라는 뜻이 있어서 get muddy 하면 '진흙탕이 되다'로 해석하면 됩니다. 이렇게 get은 상태의 변화를 나타냅니다. 그래서 is dark(어둡다) → get dark(어두워지다), is hungry(배고프다) → get hungry(배고파지다)처럼 get이 들어가면 서서히 어떠한 상태가 되어 가는 것에 초점이 맞춰집니다.

확인문제　**1**　Drink your tea before it gets cold.

2　My dog is getting fat these days.

Up 5   접속사로 길어진 문장 해석하기 – 시간 접속사 when

_{누가}   _{한다}   _{~할 때}

Most fish / move / when they're sleeping.
대부분의 물고기는   움직인다   그들이 잠을 잘 때

해설 대부분의 물고기는 잠을 잘 때 움직여요.

시간을 나타낼 때 쓰는 시간 접속사 when을 써서 특정 시점에 대해 이야기하고 있어요. 그래서 주어 Most fish가 언제 움직이는지 구체적으로 설명해요. when they're sleeping은 '그들이 잠을 자고 있을 때'라고 해석해요.

A 문장을 슬래시(/)로 끊어 읽은 후 우리말 해석을 완성하세요.

1 We were having dinner when the guests arrived.

→ 우리는 / 저녁을 먹고 있었다 / ＿＿＿＿＿＿＿＿＿＿＿＿＿＿

2 I studied Chinese hard when I moved to China.

→ 나는 공부했었다 / 중국어를 / 열심히 / ＿＿＿＿＿＿＿＿＿＿＿＿＿＿

3 Mike was doing his homework when the phone rang.

→ 마이크는 하는 중이었다 / 그의 숙제를 / ＿＿＿＿＿＿＿＿＿＿＿＿＿＿

B 우리말 문장과 일치하도록 영어문장을 알맞게 배열하세요.

1 나는 음악을 들을 때 행복하다.

(feel happy / when / I listen / I / to music)

→ ＿＿＿＿＿＿＿＿＿＿＿＿＿＿＿＿＿＿＿＿＿＿＿＿＿＿＿＿＿＿.

2 우리가 역에 도착했을 때 지하철은 떠났다.

(at the station / when / we arrived / the train / departed)

→ ＿＿＿＿＿＿＿＿＿＿＿＿＿＿＿＿＿＿＿＿＿＿＿＿＿＿＿＿＿＿.

Up 6 의문사가 포함된 의문문 해석하기 – why

무엇을

Do you know / why streams and lakes get muddy?
당신은 알고 있나요   왜 개울과 호수가 진흙탕이 되는지를

해설 당신은 개울과 호수가 왜 진흙탕이 되는지 알고 있나요?

이 문장에서 why는 이유를 묻는 의문 부사로, '개울과 호수가 왜 진흙탕이 되는지'를 묻고 있습니다. why로 시작하는 이 절은 동사 know의 목적어 역할을 하고, '당신은 ~을 알고 있나요?'로 해석할 수 있습니다.

 문장을 슬래시(/)로 끊어 읽은 후 우리말 해석을 완성하세요.

1 Do you know why the sky is blue?

→ 당신은 알고 있나요 / _______________________________

2 Do you know why people celebrate Christmas?

→ 당신은 알고 있나요 / _______________________________

3 Do you know why birds fly south in winter?

→ 당신은 알고 있나요 / _______________________________

B 우리말 문장과 일치하도록 영어문장을 알맞게 배열하세요.

1 당신은 왜 우리가 물을 마셔야 하는지 알고 있나요?

(we need to / why / do you know / drink water)

→ ____?

2 당신은 왜 식물은 햇빛이 필요한지 알고 있나요?

(plants / do you know / why / need sunlight)

→ ____?

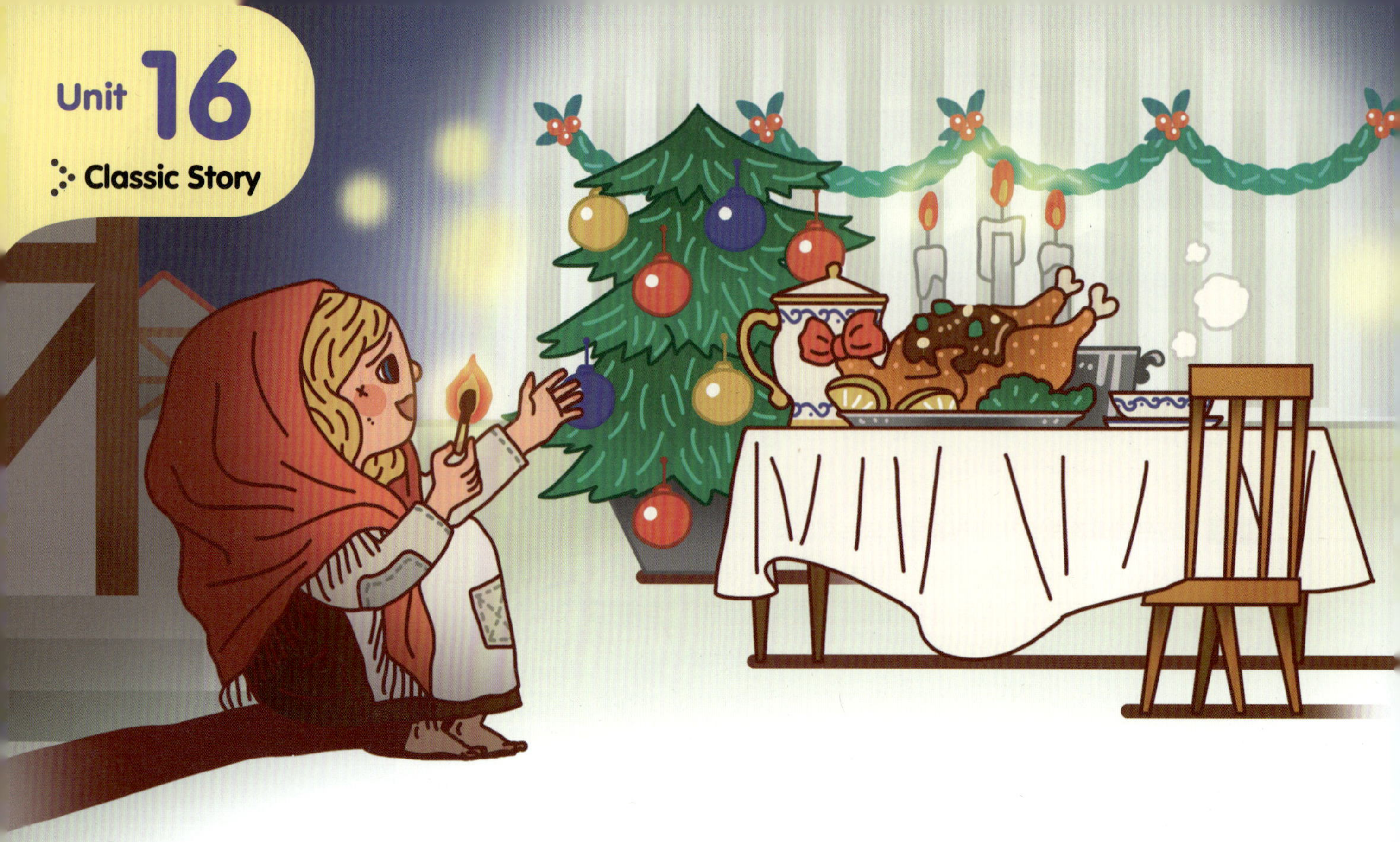

The Little Match Girl

It was a very cold night. The little match girl was leaning against a wall outside a house. She wasn't wearing a coat or shoes. She was so cold. She lit a match to warm herself.

The little match girl held the match, and she could see a warm stove in the light. Her feet were warm. But when the match went out, the stove was gone. She struck another match. She could see a table full of delicious food and a Christmas tree. But the match went out again.

She continuously lit her matches. This time she could see her dead grandmother, who loved her so much. She wanted to follow her grandmother.

- **match** 성냥
- **lean** 기대다
- **against**
  ~에 대고, 기대어
- **wall** 담, 벽
- **lit** 불을 붙였다
  (light 불을 붙이다)
- **stove** 난로
- **went out** (불이) 꺼졌다
  (go out (불이) 꺼지다)
- **gone** 사라진, 떠난
- **struck** (성냥을) 그었다
  (strike (성냥을) 긋다)
- **continuously**
  계속해서

Comprehension Check

A 문장을 읽고 옳으면 T(True), 틀리면 F(False)에 동그라미 하세요.

1 The little match girl lit a match because she was cold.　　**T / F**

2 She could see a warm stove in the light.　　**T / F**

3 She had a Christmas tree outside of her house.　　**T / F**

B 다음을 읽고 알맞은 답을 고르세요.

1 This passage is mainly about ________________.

   a a very cold night

   b a girl who had matches

   c a Christmas tree

2 When the little match girl lit the first match, what did she see?

   a A warm stove

   b Her dead grandmother

   c A table full of delicious food and a Christmas tree

3 What is true according to this story?

   a She lives with her grandmother.

   b She had many candles.

   c She didn't wear a coat.

C 문장을 완성하는 단어를 써 넣으세요.

1 The little match girl was __________ against a wall outside a house.

2 She continuously __________ her matches.

3 She wanted to __________ her grandmother.

Read and Understand

● 잘 읽고 이해했나요? 문장의 정확한 의미를 알아보세요.

1. It was a very cold night.

____

→ lean against는 '~에 대고 기대다'라는 뜻이에요.

2. The little match girl / was leaning / against a wall / outside a house.

성냥팔이 소녀는 _______________ 벽에 대고 집 밖에서

3. She wasn't wearing / a coat or shoes.   She was so cold.

그녀는 입고 있지 않았다 _______________ 그녀는 무척 추웠다

← 여기서 warm은 '따뜻한'이라는 형용사가 아니라 '따뜻하게 하다'라는 동사로 쓰였어요.

4. She lit / a match / to warm herself.

그녀는 불을 붙였다 성냥에 _______________

5. The little match girl / held the match, / and she could see /

그 성냥팔이 소녀는 _______________ 그리고 그녀는 볼 수 있었다

a warm stove / in the light.

따뜻한 난로를 불빛 속에서

6. Her feet / were warm.

그녀의 발은 _______________

7. But / when the match went out, / the stove was gone.

그러나 성냥이 꺼지자 _______________

8. She struck / another match.

그녀는 그었다 _______________

→ full of delicious food가 table을 뒤에서 꾸며주고 있어요.

9. She could see a table / full of delicious food / and a Christmas tree.

그녀는 식탁을 볼 수 있었다 _______________ 그리고 크리스마스 트리를

10. But / the match went out / again.

하지만 _______________ 다시

11. She continuously lit / her matches.

                              그녀의 성냥들을

12. This time / she could see / her dead grandmother, /

이번에는　　　　　그녀는 볼 수 있었다

 who loved her so much는 앞에 나온 grandmother를 보충 설명해 주고 있어요.

who loved her so much.

그녀를 아주 많이 사랑해 주셨던

13. She wanted to follow / her grandmother.

                              그녀의 할머니를

Grammar Point　재귀대명사 herself

본문 쏙 She lit a match to warm **herself**.

그녀는 그녀 자신을 따뜻하게 하기 위해 성냥에 불을 붙였다.

her은 '그녀를'이라는 뜻이지만 herself는 '그녀 자신'이라는 뜻이에요. herself처럼 어떤 행동에 대한 대상이 자기 자신일 때 사용하는 대명사를 '재귀대명사'라고 해요. 인칭별 재귀대명사를 알아두세요.

| myself 내 자신 | yourself 너 자신 | himself 그 자신 | herself 그녀 자신 |
| itself 그것 자신 | ourselves 우리 자신 | yourselves 너희 자신 | themselves 그들 자신 |

확인문제　**1** Don't blame yourself.

2 I enjoyed myself at the party.

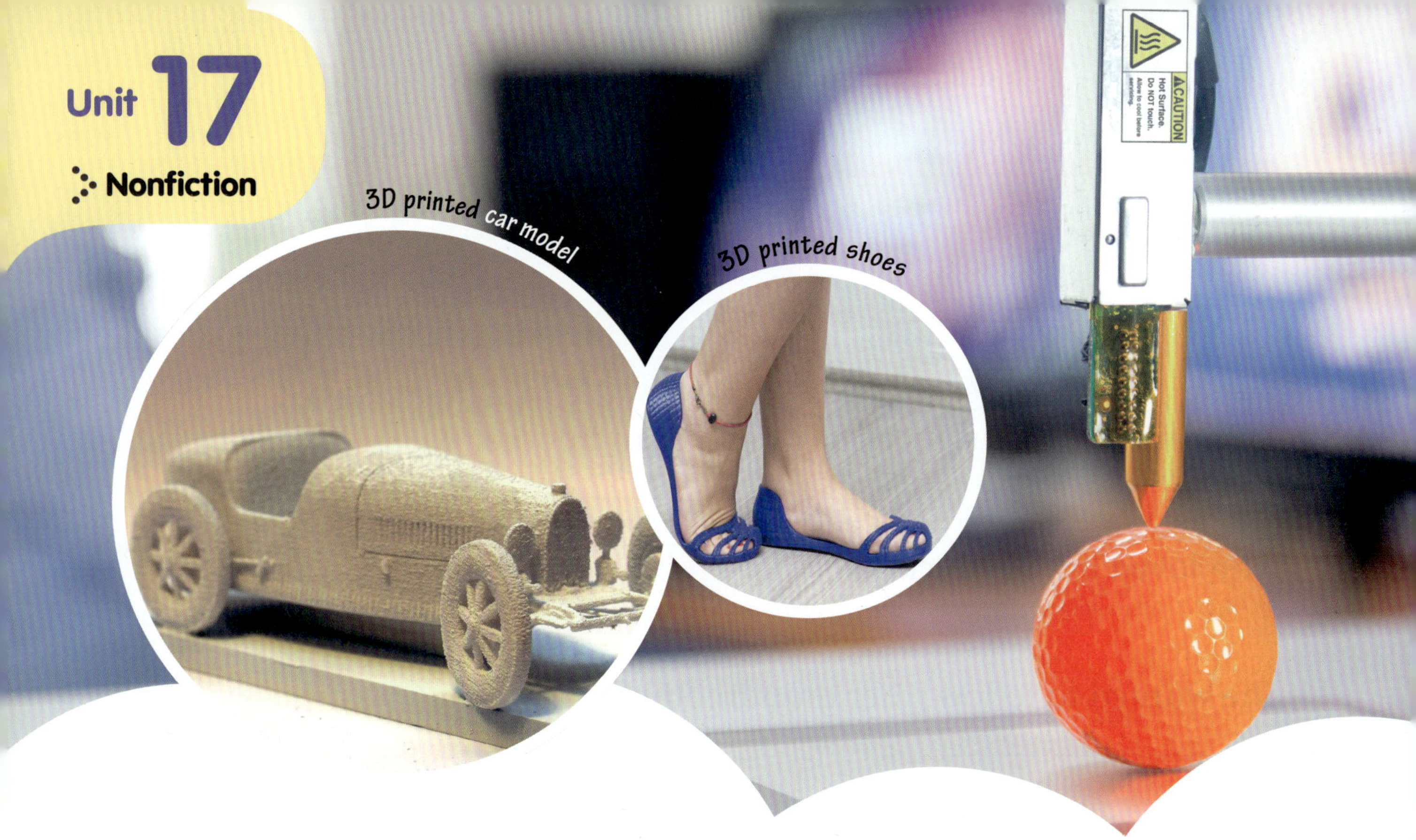

3D Printers

A 3D printer isn't like a regular printer. Instead of printing simple text on a single piece of paper, a 3D printer can print a real thing! 3D printers spray or squeeze raw materials like plastic, metal, paper, rubber, silicon, or any other kind of material which is needed to print out the things. Three-dimensional objects such as musical instruments, human body parts, shoes, cars, and even a house can be made with 3D printers.

There are many different kinds of 3D printers these days. Unfortunately, they are still too expensive for most individuals to buy and use at home. However, with 3D printers creating everything from clothing to body parts, the future appears bright for 3D printing technology.

- **instead of** ~ 대신
- **text** 글자
- **real** 실제의, 진짜의
- **squeeze** 짜내다
- **raw** 가공되지 않은
- **material** 재료
- **plastic** 플라스틱
- **metal** 금속
- **rubber** 고무
- **silicon** 실리콘
- **dimensional** 차원의
- **object** 물체
- **musical instrument** 악기
- **unfortunately** 유감스럽게도
- **individual** 개인
- **however** 하지만
- **create** 창조하다
- **appear** ~인 것 같다
- **technology** 기술

Comprehension Check

 문장을 읽고 옳으면 T(True), 틀리면 F(False)에 동그라미 하세요.

1 A 3D printer prints text on a single piece of paper.   **T / F**

2 People made human body parts with 3D printers.   **T / F**

3 There is only one kind of 3D printer these days.   **T / F**

 다음을 읽고 알맞은 답을 고르세요.

1 This passage is mainly about _______________.

    ⓐ regular printers

    ⓑ 3D printers

    ⓒ printing a piece of paper

2 How do 3D printers print out the things?

    ⓐ By spraying or squeezing raw materials

    ⓑ By printing simple text on a piece of paper

    ⓒ By cutting and gluing materials

3 Because they are _______________, individuals can't buy and use 3D printers at home.

    ⓐ too heavy   ⓑ too complicated   ⓒ too expensive

 문장을 완성하는 단어를 써 넣으세요.

1 A 3D printer isn't like a __________ printer.

2 __________ of printing simple text on a single piece of paper, a 3D printer can print a __________ thing!

3 With 3D printers __________ everything from clothing to body parts, the future appears __________ for 3D printing technology.

● 잘 읽고 이해했나요? 문장의 정확한 의미를 알아보세요.

1. A 3D printer isn't like / a regular printer.

3D 프린터는 ~같지 않다

single은 '단 하나의'라는 뜻이에요.

2. Instead of printing simple text / on a single piece of paper, /

단순한 글자를 출력하는 대신

a 3D printer can print / a real thing!

3D 프린터는 출력할 수 있다　　　　실제 물건을

raw material은 '가공되지 않은 재료'이므로 '원자재'를 뜻해요.

3. 3D printers spray or squeeze / raw materials / like plastic, metal, paper,

3D 프린터는 분사하거나 짜낸다　　　　원자재들을　　　　플라스틱, 금속, 종이,

which는 관계대명사로 which절이 material을 꾸며주고 있어요.

rubber, silicon, / or any other kind of material / which is needed /

고무, 실리콘 같은　　　　　　　　　　　　　　　　　필요한

to print out the things.

그 물건들을 출력하는 데

Three부터 house까지가 주어 부분이에요.

4. Three-dimensional objects / such as / musical instruments, human

3차원 물체들이　　　　　　　　~같은　　　　악기들, 사람의 신체 기관들,

body parts, shoes, cars, and even a house / can be made / with 3D

신발들, 자동차들, 심지어 집　　　　　　　　　　　　　3차원 프린터로

printers.

these days는 과거와 비교해서 '요즘에는, 근래에는'이라는 뜻이에요.

5. There are / many different kinds of 3D printers / these days.

있다　　　　　　　　　　　　　　　　　　　　　요즘에는

(too A to B)는 'B하기에는 너무 A하다'는 뜻이에요.

6. Unfortunately, / they are still too expensive / for most individuals /

유감스럽게도　　　　　그것들은 아직 너무 비싸다　　　　대부분의 개인들이

to buy and use at home.

7. However, / with 3D printers / creating everything /
그러나　　　　　3D프린터들로　　　　　모든 것을 만들어 내는

from clothing to body parts, / the future appears bright /
의류부터 신체 기관까지　　　　　　　　

for 3D printing technology.
3차원 출력 기술을 위한

명사(사물)를 뒤에서 꾸며주는 which절

본문 쏙　any other kind of material **which** is needed to print out the things

물건들을 출력하는 데 필요한 다른 종류의 재료

여기서 which는 앞에 나온 material에 대해 설명하기 위해 쓰인 거예요. 즉, 밑줄 친 which절이 material을 꾸며주는 것이므로 material~things를 '물건들을 출력하는 데 필요한 다른 종류의 재료'라고 해석하면 됩니다. 이런 용도로 쓰는 which를 '관계대명사'라고 하고, which 대신 that을 쓰기도 해요.

확인문제　**1** Here is the car which I wish to have.

　

2 That is the pine tree which was planted by your grandfather.

What Happens at City Hall?

Stacy is a school newspaper reporter. She wanted to write an article about City Hall. She thought, "Everyone knows where City Hall is. But do we know what happens there?"

A few days later, Stacy interviewed the mayor, Janet Duncan. The mayor's office was in City Hall.

"What do you do here?" asked Stacy.

"As the mayor, I lead the city council meetings," said Janet. "We meet regularly to make important decisions for our town."

"Can you give me an example?" asked Stacy.

"Well, imagine someone wants to open a big department store right next to an elementary school. It could be dangerous because many shoppers would drive near the school. So, we would not allow that."

"Oh, so you keep our town safe!" said Stacy.

- **newspaper** 신문
- **reporter** 기자
- **City Hall** 시청
- **interview** 인터뷰하다
- **mayor** 시장
- **office** 사무실
- **lead** 이끌다
- **city council** 시 의회
- **meeting** 회의
- **regularly** 정기적으로
- **decision** 결정
- **example** 예
- **department store** 백화점
- **elementary school** 초등학교
- **shopper** 쇼핑객

Comprehension Check

A 문장을 읽고 옳으면 T(True), 틀리면 F(False)에 동그라미 하세요.

1 Stacy wanted to write an article about the school newspaper.   **T / F**

2 Stacy interviewed the mayor.   **T / F**

3 The mayor leads the city council meetings.   **T / F**

B 다음을 읽고 알맞은 답을 고르세요.

1 This passage is mainly about ________________.

  ⓐ who lives at City Hall

  ⓑ where City Hall is

  ⓒ what happens at City Hall

2 Why does Stacy want to write an article about City Hall?

  ⓐ To know what happens there

  ⓑ To know who works there

  ⓒ To know where it is located

3 What is one of the roles the mayor fills in working for the town?

  ⓐ To lead the city council meetings to make important decisions

  ⓑ To build big department stores right next to City Hall

  ⓒ To write articles about City Hall

C 문장을 완성하는 단어를 써 넣으세요.

1 Stacy is a school newspaper ____________.

2 "Everyone knows where City Hall is. But do we know what __________ there?"

3 "It could be _________ because many shoppers would drive near the school."

● 잘 읽고 이해했나요? 문장의 정확한 의미를 알아보세요.

1. Stacy is / a school newspaper reporter.
스테이시는 ~이다 ________________________

2. She wanted / to write an article / about City Hall.
그녀는 원했다   ________________________   시청에 대한

→ everyone의 뜻은 '모든 사람'이지만, 단수로 취급해서 뒤에 오는 동사에 -s를 붙여요.

3. She thought, / "Everyone knows / where City Hall is.
그녀는 생각했다   모두 알고 있다   ________________________

4. But / do we know / what happens there?"
하지만   우리는 알고 있는가?   ________________________

5. A few days later, / Stacy interviewed / the mayor, Janet Duncan.
________________________   스테이시는 인터뷰했다   재닛 던컨 시장님을

6. The mayor's office / was in City Hall.
________________________   시청 안에 있었다

7. "What do you do / here?" / asked Stacy.
무엇을 하시나요?   여기에서   ____________

→ as는 '~로서'라는 뜻으로 자격을 말해요.

8. "As the mayor, / I lead / the city council meetings," / said Janet.
________________   나는 이끌어요   시 의회 회의들을   재닛이 말했다

→ make a decision은 '결정하다'라는 뜻이에요.

9. "We meet / regularly / to make important decisions / for our town."
우리는 만나요   정기적으로   ________________________   우리 시를 위해서

→ give an example은 '예를 들다'라는 뜻이에요.

10. "Can you give me an example?" / asked Stacy.
________________________________   스테이시가 물었다

11. "Well, / imagine / someone wants / to open a big department store /
음   상상해 보세요   누군가 원한다고   대형 백화점을 여는 것을

→ right에는 '바로'라는 뜻이 있어요. 그래서 right next to는 '바로 ~ 옆에'라는 뜻이에요.

right next to an elementary school.

━━━━━━━━━━━━━━━━━━━━━━

↱ 조동사인 could나 would 뒤에는 항상 동사원형을 써요.

12. It could be dangerous / because / many shoppers would drive /
          왜냐하면   많은 쇼핑객들이 운전할 거예요

near the school.
학교 근처에서

13. So, / we would not allow / that."
그래서 ━━━━━━━━━━━━━━━ 그것을

14. "Oh, so you keep / our town safe!" / said Stacy.
와, 그러니까 시장님은 지켜 주시는군요 ━━━━━━━━━ 스테이시가 말했다

알아두면 문장이 쉽게
이해되는 그래머 포인트

Grammar Point **where 주어+동사**

본문 쏙   Everyone knows where City Hall is.
모두 시청이 어디 있는지 알고 있다.

where City Hall is는 '시청이 어디에 있는지'라는 뜻이고, know의 목적어로 쓰였어요. 이렇게 〈where 주어+동사〉는 '~이 어디에 ~하는지'라고 해석하면 됩니다. 이런 경우에는 where 뒤에 '동사 +주어'가 아니라 '주어+동사'의 순서로 쓴다는 점을 주의하세요.

확인문제   **1**   She knows where the restaurant is.

      2   I know where he lives.

The Earth Is Spinning

Did you know that you are moving right now? That's right! In Korea, the ground below you is moving at almost 1,300 kilometers per hour! And it's taking you with it!

The earth is spinning. Put a marble on a smooth table. Spin it. That's what the earth is doing. Of course, we don't feel this movement. To us, it seems like the sun is moving. That's why we say the sun "rises" in the morning and "sets" at night. Actually, the sun doesn't move.

As our side of the earth moves toward the sun, we have daytime. When it moves away, we have night. The earth takes 24 hours to complete one spin. That's why one day is 24 hours long!

- **below** 아래에
- **per** ~당, 마다
- **spin** 돌다; 회전
- **marble** 구슬
- **smooth** 매끄러운
- **movement** 움직임
- **seem** ~인 것 같다
- **rise** (해가) 뜨다
- **set** (해가) 지다
- **actually** 사실은, 실제로
- **toward** ~쪽으로, ~을 향해
- **complete** 완료하다

Comprehension Check

A 문장을 읽고 옳으면 T(True), 틀리면 F(False)에 동그라미 하세요.

1 The ground below you is moving.　　　　　　T / F

2 We feel the earth's movement.　　　　　　T / F

3 The sun takes 24 hours to complete one spin.　　T / F

B 다음을 읽고 알맞은 답을 고르세요.

1 This passage is mainly about _______________.

　ⓐ daytime

　ⓑ the movement of the earth

　ⓒ the movement of the sun

2 How does day and night come?

　ⓐ Because the sun is spinning.

　ⓑ Because the sun is moving around the earth.

　ⓒ Because the earth spins as it moves around the sun.

3 According to the story, what is true?

　ⓐ The earth takes 24 days to complete one spin.

　ⓑ In Korea, the ground is moving at almost 1,300 kilometers per hour.

　ⓒ When the earth spins away from the sun, we have daytime.

C 문장을 완성하는 단어를 써 넣으세요.

1 That's what the earth is __________.

2 To us, it seems like the __________ is moving.

3 The earth takes 24 hours to __________ one spin.

● 잘 읽고 이해했나요? 문장의 정확한 의미를 알아보세요.

1. Did you know / that you are moving / right now?

여러분은 알고 있었는가?　　　　＿＿＿＿＿＿＿＿＿＿　지금 이 순간

2. That's right!　In Korea, / the ground below you / is moving /

맞다　　　　　　한국에서　　　＿＿＿＿＿＿＿＿＿＿　움직이고 있다

> per는 '~당, ~마다'의 뜻으로, per hour는 '시간당, 시속'이라는 뜻이에요.

at almost 1,300 kilometers / per hour!

거의 1,300 킬로미터로　　　　　　　한 시간에

> '그것은 그것과 함께 여러분을 데리고 가다', 즉 '그것과 함께 여러분이 움직이고 있다'는 뜻이에요.

3. And / it's taking you / with it!

그리고　＿＿＿＿＿＿＿＿＿＿　그것과 함께!

4. The earth is spinning.　Put a marble / on a smooth table.

지구는 돌고 있다　　　　　　구슬을 놓아라　　　＿＿＿＿＿＿＿＿＿＿.

> 〈what 주어+동사〉는 '(주어)가 ~하는 것'이라고 해석해요.

5. Spin it.　That's / what the earth is doing.

그것을 돌려라　그것이 ~이다　＿＿＿＿＿＿＿＿＿＿

6. Of course, / we don't feel / this movement.

물론　　　　　우리는 느끼지 않는다　　＿＿＿＿＿＿＿＿

> seem like는 '~처럼 보인다, ~인 것 같다'라는 뜻이에요.

7. To us, / it seems like / the sun is moving.

우리에게는　그것은 ~처럼 보인다　　＿＿＿＿＿＿＿＿

8. That's why / we say / the sun "rises" in the morning /

그래서　　　　우리는 말한다　　＿＿＿＿＿＿＿＿＿＿＿＿＿＿

and "sets" at night.

그리고 밤에는 "진다"고

9. Actually, / the sun doesn't move.

사실　　　　＿＿＿＿＿＿＿＿＿＿

10. As / our side of the earth / moves toward the sun, / we have daytime.

~하면서   지구에서 우리가 있는 쪽이   우리는 낮을 가진다

11. When it moves away, / we have night.

우리는 밤을 가진다

12. The earth / takes 24 hours / to complete one spin.

지구는   24시간이 걸린다

13. That's why one day is 24 hours long!

 That's what...

본문 쏙 That's what the earth is doing.

그것이 지구가 하고 있는 것이다.

〈what 주어+동사〉 형태는 '(주어)가 ~하는 것'이라는 뜻이에요. 따라서 〈That's what 주어+동사〉는 '그것이 (주어)가 ~하는 것이다'라는 뜻이에요. 결국 이 문장은 '그것이 지구가 하고 있는 것이다'라고 해석하면 됩니다. 〈That's why 주어+동사〉는 '그것이 (주어)가 ~하는 이유다'라는 뜻이고, 〈That's how 주어+동사〉는 '그것이 (주어)가 ~하는 방법이다'라는 뜻이라는 것도 함께 알아두세요.

확인문제 **1** That's what I need.

2 That's what I want to talk about.

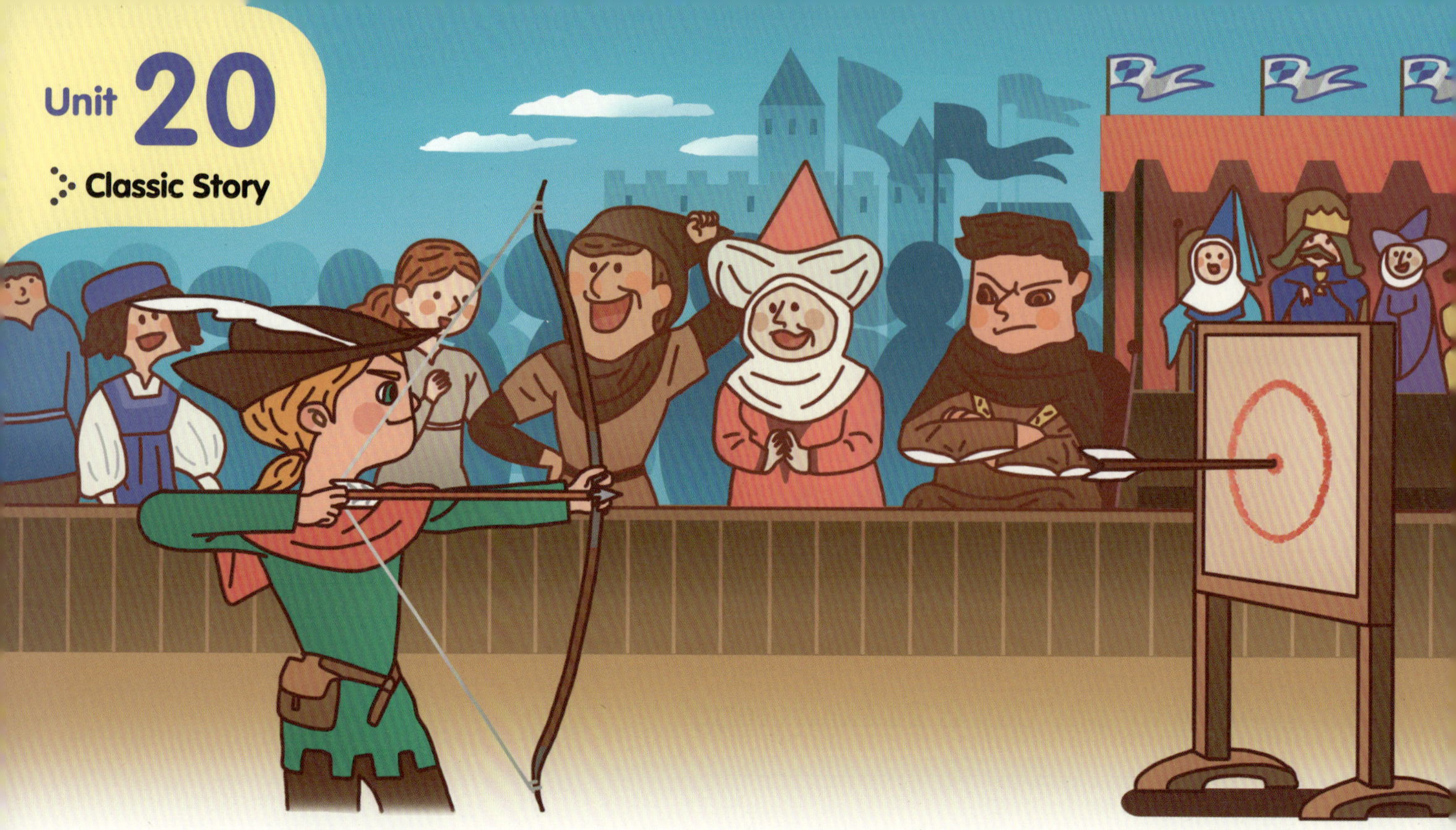

Robin Hood

Robin Hood was a man who lived in Sherwood Forest in England. He robbed the rich and gave to the poor. That made the rich scared of going through Sherwood Forest. They knew Robin Hood would attack them.

One day, the sheriff wanted to catch Robin Hood, so he made a plan. He held a competition to choose the best archer in town. The sheriff knew that Robin Hood would come to the competition because he was a good archer.

A man in green clothes was the last person to shoot for the first prize. The arrow went through the bullseye, and another two arrows hit the sheriff's chair. It was Robin Hood.

- **rob** 도둑질하다
- **go through** 통과하다, 지나가다
- **attack** 공격하다
- **sheriff** 주 장관, 보안관
- **catch** 잡다
- **plan** 계획
- **competition** 대회
- **choose** 뽑다, 선택하다
- **archer** 활 쏘는 사람(궁수)
- **prize** 상, 상품
- **bullseye** 과녁의 중심
- **hit** 맞혔다 (hit 맞히다)

A 문장을 읽고 옳으면 T(True), 틀리면 F(False)에 동그라미 하세요.

1 Robin Hood lived in Sherwood Forest in America.   **T / F**

2 Robin Hood robbed the rich and gave to the poor.   **T / F**

3 A man in green clothes was Robin Hood.   **T / F**

B 다음을 읽고 알맞은 답을 고르세요.

1 This passage is mainly about ________________.

   ⓐ the competition

   ⓑ Robin Hood

   ⓒ Sherwood Forest

2 Why did the sheriff hold a competition to choose the best archer?

   ⓐ Because he wanted to rob the rich.

   ⓑ Because he wanted to catch Robin Hood.

   ⓒ Because he wanted to get first prize.

3 Why were the rich scared of going through Sherwood Forest?

   ⓐ Because there were scary animals in the forest.

   ⓑ Because Robin Hood would attack them.

   ⓒ Because the sheriff lived in Sherwood Forest.

C 문장을 완성하는 단어를 써 넣으세요.

1 The __________ wanted to catch Robin Hood, so he made a __________.

2 A man in green clothes was the last person to _________ for the first prize.

3 The arrow went through the __________.

● 잘 읽고 이해했나요? 문장의 정확한 의미를 알아보세요.

1. Robin Hood was a man / who lived in Sherwood Forest / in England.
로빈 후드는 남자였다 _______________________________________ 영국의

→ the rich는 '부자들', the poor는 '가난한 사람들'이라는 뜻이에요.

2. He robbed / the rich / and gave / to the poor.
그는 도둑질했다   부자들을   그리고 주었다 ____________

3. That made / the rich / scared of / going through Sherwood Forest.
그것이 만들었다   부자들을   두려워하게 ________________________

→ Robin ~ them은 knew의 목적어인데, 이 목적절을 이끄는 that이 생략된 형태예요.

4. They knew / Robin Hood would attack them.
그들은 알았다 _____________________________

5. One day, / the sheriff wanted to catch / Robin Hood, /
어느 날 ___________________________ 로빈 후드를

so he made a plan.
그래서 그는 계획을 세웠다

→ hold a competition은 '대회를 개최하다/열다'라는 뜻이고, held는 hold의 과거형이에요.

6. He held a competition / to choose the best archer / in town.
그는 대회를 열었다 ___________________________ 마을에서

7. The sheriff knew / that Robin Hood would come / to the competition /
장관은 알았다 ___________________________ 대회에

because / he was a good archer.
왜냐하면   그는 훌륭한 궁수였다

8. A man in green clothes / was the last person / to shoot /
___________________________ 마지막 사람이었다   활을 쏠

for the first prize.
1등 상을 위해

9. The arrow went through / the bullseye, / and another two arrows hit /

　　　과녁의 중앙을　　　그리고 또 다른 두 개의 화살은 맞혔다

the sheriff's chair.

장관의 의자를

10. It was Robin Hood.

Grammar Point 명사(사람)를 뒤에서 꾸며주는 **who**절

본문 쏙 Robin Hood was a <u>man</u> <u>who lived in Sherwood Forest in England</u>.

로빈 후드는 영국의 셔우드 숲에 사는 남자였다.

여기서 who는 앞에 나온 a man에 대해 설명하기 위해 쓰인 거예요. 즉, 밑줄 친 who절이 man을 꾸며주는 것이므로 a man ~ England를 '영국의 셔우드 숲에 사는 남자'라고 해석하면 됩니다. 앞에서 배운 관계대명사 which와 같은 용법인데, 여기서는 사람인 a man을 수식하기 때문에 who를 쓴 거예요.

확인문제 **1** Kevin is a man who is tall and smart.

　

2 There are five boys who want to play basketball.

Up 7 접속사로 길어진 문장 해석하기 – because

무엇이 ~하다 / ~때문에

It could be dangerous / because many shoppers would drive near the school.

그것은 위험할 수 있어요 / 많은 쇼핑객들이 운전하기 때문에 / 학교 근처에서

해설 많은 쇼핑객들이 학교 근처에서 운전을 할 테니 그것은 위험할 수 있어요.

접속사 because로 시작하는 절은 앞에 오는 문장에 대한 원인이나 이유를 설명하는 역할을 합니다. 이 문장에서는 그것이 위험할 수 있는 이유로 '많은 쇼핑객들이 학교 근처에서 운전하기 때문'이라고 설명하고 있습니다.

A 문장을 슬래시(/)로 끊어 읽은 후 우리말 해석을 완성하세요.

1 It could be dangerous because the rain made the road slippery.

→ 그것은 위험할 수 있어요 / ____

2 It could be quiet because everyone left one hour ago.

→ 그것은 조용할 수 있어요 / _______________________ / 한 시간 전에

3 It could be fun because we are going to have a picnic at the park.

→ 그것은 재미있을 수 있어요 / _______________________ / 공원에

B 우리말 문장과 일치하도록 영어문장을 알맞게 배열하세요.

1 내가 수프에 소금을 많이 넣어서 짤 수 있어요.

(to the soup / because / It could be salty / I added too much salt)

→ ____.

2 우리가 긴 거리를 걸어야 해서 피곤할 수 있어요.

(because / It could be tiring / we have to walk / a long distance)

→ ____.

Up 8 관계대명사로 길어진 문장 해석하기 – who

누구는   ~이다   어떠한

Robin Hood / **was a man** / **who lived in Sherwood forest in England.**

로빈 후드는   남자였다   영국의 셔우드 숲에 사는

해설 로빈 후드는 영국의 셔우드 숲에 사는 남자였어요.

2형식(주어+동사+보어) 문장인데, 보어 a man을 수식하는 who 관계대명사절이 붙어 길어진 문장이에요. who lived in Sherwood forest in England는 the man을 보충 설명하여 '영국의 셔우드 숲에 사는 사람'이라는 의미를 만듭니다. who 는 사람을 지칭하는 관계대명사입니다.

A 문장을 슬래시(/)로 끊어 읽은 후 우리말 해석을 완성하세요.

1 He is a teacher who teaches math in a fun and exciting way.

→ 그는 선생님이다 / _________________________ / 재미있고 흥미로운 방법으로

2 My friend is a doctor who helps children in need.

→ 내 친구는 의사다 / _________________________ / 도움이 필요한

3 They are the players who won the baseball game last weekend.

→ 그들은 그 선수들이다 / _________________________ / 지난 주말에

B 우리말 문장과 일치하도록 영어문장을 알맞게 배열하세요.

1 그녀는 옆집에 사는 친절한 이웃이에요.

(is the kind neighbor / who lives next door / she)

→ ____.

2 그 소녀는 그 파티에서 노래한 가수예요.

(who sang / at the party / is the singer / the girl)

→ ____.

Key Words 200

이 책으로 200개 필수 어휘를 마스터 했어!

A

- [ ] **across** 가로질러
- [ ] **active** 활동적인
- [ ] **adventure** 모험
- [ ] **after all** 결국
- [ ] **against** ~에 대고, 기대어
- [ ] **always** 항상
- [ ] **ancient** 고대의
- [ ] **another** 또 다른
- [ ] **area** 지역
- [ ] **arrow** 화살
- [ ] **as well as** ~뿐만 아니라
- [ ] **attack** 공격하다
- [ ] **audience** 관중, 청중

B

- [ ] **back** 뒤쪽
- [ ] **backwards** 뒤로
- [ ] **balance** 균형을 잡다
- [ ] **beauty** 아름다움
- [ ] **begin** 시작하다 (과거형 began)
- [ ] **below** 아래에
- [ ] **bent** 굽히다 (과거형 bent)
- [ ] **beside** 옆에
- [ ] **blanket** 담요
- [ ] **board** 칠판, 판자
- [ ] **bother** 방해하다
- [ ] **bow** 활
- [ ] **bridge** 다리
- [ ] **bring** 가져오다 (과거형 brought)
- [ ] **bury** (보이지 않게) 묻다

C

- [ ] **catch** 잡다
- [ ] **caught** 잡았다
- [ ] **celebrate** 기념하다
- [ ] **check on** ~을 확인하다
- [ ] **choose** 뽑다, 선택하다
- [ ] **clam** 조개
- [ ] **claw** 발톱
- [ ] **climb up** ~에 오르다
- [ ] **closet** 옷장
- [ ] **coastline** 해안선
- [ ] **coin** 동전
- [ ] **collect** 모으다
- [ ] **communicate** 의사소통을 하다
- [ ] **competition** 대회
- [ ] **complete** 완료하다
- [ ] **contain** 담고 있다
- [ ] **continuously** 계속해서
- [ ] **cough** 기침
- [ ] **country** 나라
- [ ] **crop** 농작물
- [ ] **cross** 건너다
- [ ] **crowd** 군중
- [ ] **crowded** 붐비는
- [ ] **crown** 왕위에 앉히다
- [ ] **curiosity** 호기심

D

- [ ] **decision** 결정
- [ ] **develop** 개발하다
- [ ] **dream** 꿈; 꿈을 꾸다

E

- [ ] **eel** 장어
- [ ] **electric** 전기의
- [ ] **emotion** 감정

- ☐ **England** 영국
- ☐ **entire** 전체의
- ☐ **erosion** 침식
- ☐ **establish** 설립하다
- ☐ **example** 예
- ☐ **exception** 예외
- ☐ **explore** 탐험하다
- ☐ **express** 표현하다
- ☐ **eyelid** 눈꺼풀

F

- ☐ **fail** 실패하다
- ☐ **fantastic** 환상적인
- ☐ **fear** 두려움
- ☐ **feed** 먹이를 먹이다 (과거형 fed)
- ☐ **fight** 싸우다
- ☐ **film** 영화; 촬영하다
- ☐ **finally** 마침내
- ☐ **flat** 납작한
- ☐ **flu** 독감
- ☐ **fought** 싸웠다
- ☐ **from now on** 앞으로는

G

- ☐ **gather** 모이다
- ☐ **gill** 아가미
- ☐ **go through** 통과하다, 지나가다
- ☐ **god** 신
- ☐ **goddess** 여신
- ☐ **gone** 사라진, 떠난

- ☐ **Greek** 그리스어

H

- ☐ **harvest** 수확하다; 수확
- ☐ **hit** 맞히다 (과거형 hit)
- ☐ **hold** (손에) 들다 (과거형 held)
- ☐ **human** 인간, 사람

I

- ☐ **identify** 알아보다
- ☐ **imagination** 상상
- ☐ **impress** 감동[감명]을 주다
- ☐ **individual** 개인
- ☐ **injured** 부상당한
- ☐ **injury** 부상, 상처
- ☐ **interview** 인터뷰하다
- ☐ **invite** 초대하다

J

- ☐ **jellyfish** 해파리

K

- ☐ **kind** 종류
- ☐ **knight** (중세의) 기사

L

- ☐ **lamp** 램프
- ☐ **landmark** 랜드마크

- ☐ **landscape** 풍경
- ☐ **lead** 이끌다
- ☐ **lean** 기대다
- ☐ **life** 생명체
- ☐ **lit** 불을 붙이다 (과거형 lit)
- ☐ **lizard** 도마뱀
- ☐ **lobster** 바닷가재
- ☐ **lung** 허파

M

- ☐ **marble** 구슬
- ☐ **match** 성냥
- ☐ **material** 재료
- ☐ **mayor** 시장
- ☐ **medicine** 약
- ☐ **meeting** 회의
- ☐ **messy** 지저분한
- ☐ **metal** 금속
- ☐ **might** ~할지도 모른다
- ☐ **movement** 움직임
- ☐ **muddy** 진흙투성이인
- ☐ **myth** 신화

N

- ☐ **newspaper** 신문
- ☐ **November** 11월

O

- ☐ **object** 물체
- ☐ **office** 사무실

☐ **orchard** 과수원
☐ **oval** 타원형
☐ **over** ~ 위로
☐ **owner** 주인

P

☐ **peak** 산꼭대기
☐ **pebble** 자갈
☐ **pick up** 집어 들다
☐ **piece** 일부, 부품
☐ **plan** 계획
☐ **plastic** 플라스틱
☐ **poison** 독
☐ **prize** 상, 상품
☐ **produce** 제작하다
☐ **pull** 뽑다, 당기다
☐ **pumpkin** 호박

R

☐ **railroad** 철로
☐ **rainstorm** 폭풍우
☐ **real** 실제의, 진짜의
☐ **reason** 이유
☐ **regularly** 정기적으로
☐ **reporter** 기자
☐ **rip** 찢다
☐ **rise** (해가) 뜨다
☐ **rob** 도둑질하다
☐ **Roman** 로마의
☐ **rubber** 고무
☐ **runny nose** 콧물

S

☐ **save** 구하다
☐ **scientific** 과학적인
☐ **search** 찾다, 살펴보다
☐ **seed** 씨앗
☐ **seem** ~인 것 같다
☐ **set** (해가) 지다
☐ **shark** 상어
☐ **sheriff** 주 장관
☐ **shoot** 쏘다
☐ **shot** 쐈다
☐ **shrimp** 새우
☐ **sign** 신호, 징후
☐ **smooth** 매끄러운
☐ **soldier** 군인
☐ **someday** 언젠가
☐ **species** (생물) 종
☐ **spend** (시간을) 보내다
☐ **spin** 돌다; 회전
☐ **squeeze** 짜내다
☐ **starve** 굶주리다
☐ **strike** (성냥을) 긋다
(과거형 struck)
☐ **stone** 돌
☐ **stove** 난로
☐ **stuff** 물건
☐ **succeed** 성공하다
☐ **successful** 성공적인
☐ **surface** 표면
☐ **swing** 휙 움직이다
☐ **sword** 검

T

☐ **take care of** ~를 돌보다
☐ **technology** 기술
☐ **teeth** 이빨들
☐ **text** 글자
☐ **tool** 도구
☐ **tourist** 관광객
☐ **toward** ~쪽으로, ~을 향해
☐ **trap** 덫
☐ **treatment** 치료

U

☐ **uncle** 삼촌
☐ **useful** 유용한

V

☐ **valley** 계곡
☐ **vehicle** 차량
☐ **vet** 수의사

W

☐ **wall** 담, 벽
☐ **weapon** 무기
☐ **went out** (불이) 꺼졌다
☐ **wet** 젖은
☐ **wonder** 궁금해하다

MEMO

영어 독해를 완성하는 기적 시리즈

끊어 읽기 연습으로 정확한 독해 완성하기!

기적의 직독직해

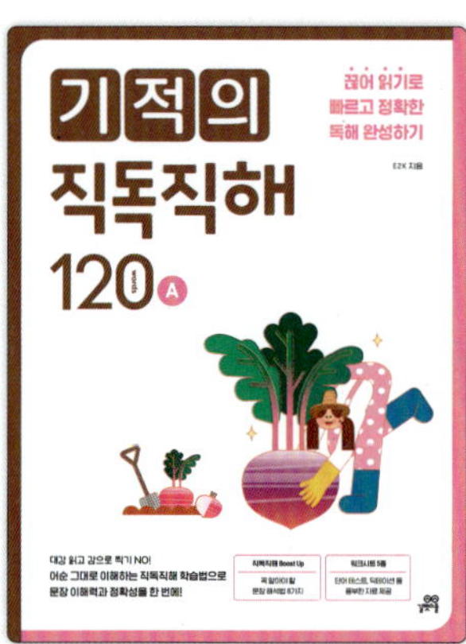

끊어 읽는 직독직해 연습으로
영어 이해력, 읽기 속도, 정확성을 동시에 키웁니다.

- 직독직해가 술술 되는 '그래머 포인트'와 '문장 해석법'
- 다양한 장르의 흥미로운 글감을 골고루!
- 단어 연습과 지문 복습을 위한 워크북 제공

전 4권 구성 | 대상: 초등 4~6학년
E2K 지음 | 각 권 168쪽 | 각 권 16,000원 | MP3, 워크시트 5종 다운로드

초등영어 핵심패턴으로 리딩 감각 키우기!

기적의 패턴리딩

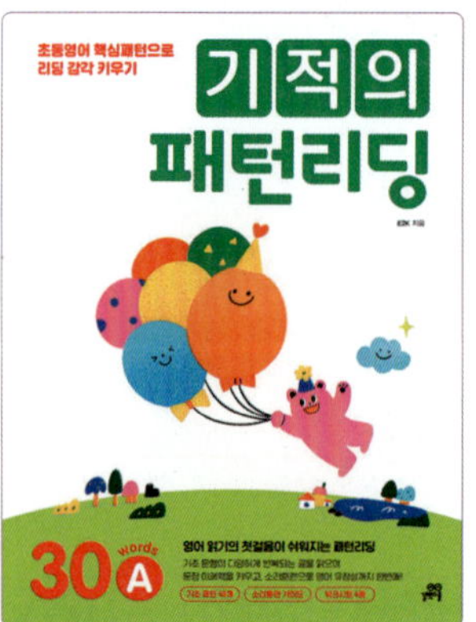

반복 문형이 등장하는 지문 읽기를 통해
어휘와 문형을 자연스럽게 습득합니다.

- 반복되는 간결한 문형으로 리딩의 시작을 쉽게
- 다양한 장르의 흥미로운 글감을 골고루!
- 단어와 지문 복습을 위한 워크북 제공

전 6권 구성 | 대상: 초등 2~4학년
E2K 지음 | 각 권 140쪽 | 각 권 16,000원 | MP3, 워크시트 4종 다운로드

기적 영어 학습서

기본이 탄탄! 실전에서 척척!
유초등 필수 영어능력을 길러주는 코어 학습서

유아 영어

재미있는 액티비티가 가득한
4~6세를 위한 영어 워크북

4세 이상

5세 이상

6세 이상

6세 이상

파닉스 완성 프로그램

알파벳 음가 → 사이트 워드
→ 읽기 연습까지!
리딩을 위한 탄탄한 기초 만들기

6세 이상 전 3권

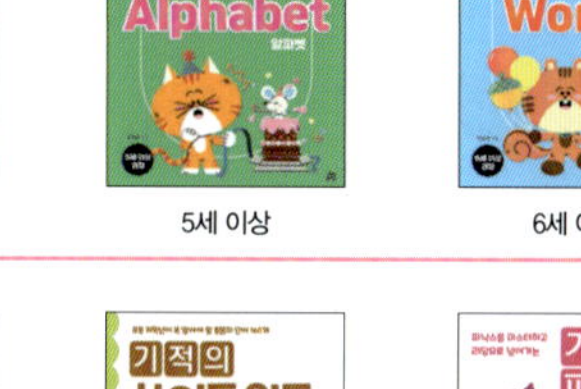

1~3학년

1~3학년 전 3권

영어 단어

영어 실력의 가장 큰 바탕은 어휘력!
교과과정 필수 어휘 익히기

3학년 이상 전 2권

1~2학년 전 2권

3~4학년 전 2권

5~6학년 전 2권

영어 리딩

패턴 문장 리딩으로 시작해
정확한 해석을 위한 끊어 읽기까지!
탄탄한 독해 실력 쌓기

2~3학년 전 3권

3~4학년 전 3권

4~5학년 전 2권

5~6학년 전 2권

5~6학년 전 2권

영어 라이팅

저학년은 패턴 영작으로,
고학년은 5형식 문장 만들기 연습으로
튼튼한 영작 실력 완성

2학년 이상 전 4권

4학년 이상 전 5권

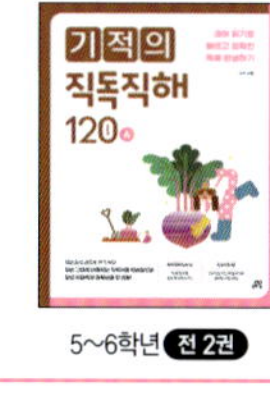

5학년 이상 전 2권

6학년 이상

영어일기

한 줄 쓰기부터 생활일기,
주제일기까지!
영어 글쓰기 실력을 키우는 시리즈

3학년 이상

4~5학년

5~6학년

영문법

중학 영어 대비, 영어 구사
정확성을 키워주는 영문법 학습

4~5학년 전 2권

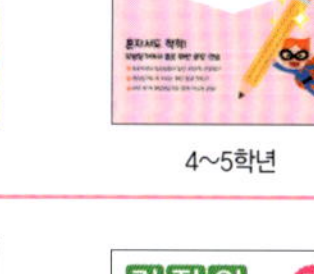

5~6학년 전 3권

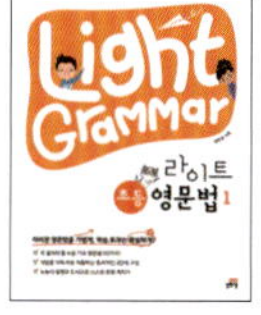

6학년 이상

기적의 직독직해

끊어 읽기로
빠르고 정확한
독해 완성하기

120 words A

Workbook & Answers
워크북 및 정답

길벗스쿨

기적의 직독직해

120 words A

Workbook

What Tails Can Do

A 우리말 뜻을 쓰고, 영단어를 세 번 쓰면서 철자를 익히세요.

1 swing	휙 움직이다	swing	swing	swing
2 lizard				
3 weapon				
4 poison				
5 balance				
6 communicate				
7 express				
8 emotion				
9 fear				
10 owner				

B 우리말 뜻에 알맞은 영단어를 연결하세요.

1 무기 ●	ⓐ owner	**6** 표현하다 ●	ⓕ communicate
2 감정 ●	ⓑ poison	**7** 휙 움직이다 ●	ⓖ express
3 주인 ●	ⓒ weapon	**8** 의사소통 하다 ●	ⓗ swing
4 독 ●	ⓓ lizard	**9** 균형을 잡다 ●	ⓘ fear
5 도마뱀 ●	ⓔ emotion	**10** 두려움 ●	ⓙ balance

C 지문을 다시 읽으며 올바른 단어에 동그라미 하세요.

What Tails Can Do

Animals use **1**(its / their) tails in many different ways. Some animals, like monkeys, use their tails to **2**(swing / swim) from tree to tree. Some animals, like **3**(squirrels / lizards), use their tails for self-defense. Scorpions use their tails as a **4**(weapon / hand). It has **5**(water / poison) in it. Fish use their tails to move through water. Kangaroos and squirrels use their tails to help themselves **6**(balance / sleep). Birds use their tails to help themselves **7**(sit / fly) in the sky.

Cats and dogs use their tails to **8**(swing / communicate). They can use their tails to **9**(impress / express) many emotions such as fear and **10**(exciting / excitement). Dogs wag their tails to **11**(greet / great) their owners.

Do you have a pet **12**(with / by) a tail? If you do, how does the pet use its tail?

Stay Healthy, Alpo

A 우리말 뜻을 쓰고, 영단어를 세 번 쓰면서 철자를 익히세요.

1	runny nose	콧물	runny nose	runny nose	runny nose
2	cough				
3	vet				
4	flu				
5	medicine				
6	take care of				
7	blanket				
8	fed				
9	wet				
10	beside				

B 우리말 뜻에 알맞은 영단어를 연결하세요.

1 콧물 •	**ⓐ** take care of		**6** 옆에 •	**ⓕ** medicine
2 독감 •	**ⓑ** fed		**7** 약 •	**ⓖ** vet
3 먹이를 줬다 •	**ⓒ** wet		**8** 수의사 •	**ⓗ** beside
4 ~를 돌보다 •	**ⓓ** runny nose		**9** 기침 •	**ⓘ** blanket
5 젖은 •	**ⓔ** flu		**10** 담요 •	**ⓙ** cough

C   지문을 다시 읽으며 올바른 단어에 동그라미 하세요.

Stay Healthy, Alpo

Yesterday morning, Alpo **1**(don't / didn't) eat or move. He had a **2**(running / runny) nose and a cough. Dad and I **3**(taked / took) Alpo to the animal hospital. The vet said he had the **4**(plu / flu). The vet also said to keep him **5**(outside / inside) and give him **6**(medicine / blanket) for a few days. Dad said that **7**(when / since) I was Alpo's big brother, it was my job to take good care of him.

Back at home, I put a clean **8**(medicine / blanket) under Alpo. I gave him water and medicine. I **9**(feeded / fed) him regularly. I kept him warm. I looked **10**(before / after) Alpo all day. I fell **11**(sleep / asleep) beside Alpo's house.

This morning, **12**(wet something / something wet) woke me up. It was Alpo! Alpo looked great! I love you, Alpo!

Florence Nightingale

A 우리말 뜻을 쓰고, 영단어를 세 번 쓰면서 철자를 익히세요.

1 England	영국	England	England	England
2 treatment				
3 injured				
4 soldier				
5 crowded				
6 injury				
7 lamp				
8 check on				
9 reason				
10 establish				

B 우리말 뜻에 알맞은 영단어를 연결하세요.

1 군인 ●	● **ⓐ** England	**6** 부상당한 ● ● **ⓕ** reason
2 부상, 상처 ●	● **ⓑ** crowded	**7** 치료 ● ● **ⓖ** check on
3 영국 ●	● **ⓒ** soldier	**8** 설립하다 ● ● **ⓗ** treatment
4 램프 ●	● **ⓓ** injury	**9** ~을 확인하다 ● ● **ⓘ** injured
5 붐비는 ●	● **ⓔ** lamp	**10** 이유 ● ● **ⓙ** establish

C 지문을 다시 읽으며 올바른 단어에 동그라미 하세요.

Florence Nightingale

1(On / In) 1845, Florence Nightingale **2**(became / established) a nurse in England. Years later, she **3**(reads / read) about the poor treatment of sick and **4**(injured / injuries) soldiers in the Crimean War. She went to Crimea and found dirty and crowded hospitals. She knew that more soldiers **5**(dead / died) from diseases than from **6**(injured / injuries) in the war.

She worked hard to clean the hospital and take care of the injured soldiers. Florence walked around the hospital in the **7**(evening / evenings), carrying a lamp and **8**(check / checking) on the injured soldiers. **9**(Of / For) this reason, many soldiers called her "The Lady with the Lamp." **10**(Thanks / Welcome) to her, **11**(more / fewer) soldiers died from diseases.

Florence **12**(became / established) the Nightingale School for nurses. She was the best nurse in the world.

The Lion and the Mouse

A 우리말 뜻을 쓰고, 영단어를 세 번 쓰면서 철자를 익히세요.

1	began	시작했다	began	began	began
2	climb up				
3	bother				
4	caught				
5	claw				
6	someday				
7	trap				
8	teeth				
9	save				
10	after all				

B 우리말 뜻에 알맞은 영단어를 연결하세요.

1 결국 ●		ⓐ caught
2 방해하다 ●		ⓑ bother
3 구하다 ●		ⓒ after all
4 잡았다 ●		ⓓ save
5 덫 ●		ⓔ trap

6 시작했다 ●		ⓕ teeth
7 ~에 오르다 ●		ⓖ began
8 이빨들 ●		ⓗ climb up
9 언젠가 ●		ⓘ claw
10 발톱 ●		ⓙ someday

C 지문을 다시 읽으며 올바른 단어에 동그라미 하세요.

The Lion and the Mouse

A little mouse began climbing up a brown hill and **1**(slide / slid) down. But the hill was a **2**(sleeping / sleepy) lion's back! **3**(Bothered / Caught) by the mouse, the lion woke up. The angry lion caught the mouse **4**(between / behind) his claws.

"Please **5**(do / let) me go. Then I'll come back and help you someday," said the mouse.

The lion laughed, "You are so tiny! How can a tiny mouse help me?" But the lion let the little mouse **6**(go / to go) because he could laugh **7**(thank / thanks) to the mouse.

The next day, the lion **8**(caught / was caught) in a trap. The mouse came to him and **9**(begin / began) to cut the rope with his **10**(toothes / teeth). Finally, the lion could get out of the trap.

"Dear friend, you saved me **11**(at / after) all. Thank you," said the lion.

"I'm **12**(glad / sorry) I could help you," said the mouse.

Bridges Around the World

A 우리말 뜻을 쓰고, 영단어를 세 번 쓰면서 철자를 익히세요.

1	bridge	다리 bridge	bridge	bridge
2	over			
3	railroad			
4	vehicle			
5	cross			
6	landmark			
7	tourist			
8	another			
9	across			
10	as well as			

B 우리말 뜻에 알맞은 영단어를 연결하세요.

1 또 다른 •   **ⓐ** as well as   **6** 랜드마크 •   **ⓕ** railroad

2 건너다 •   **ⓑ** cross   **7** 철로 •   **ⓖ** tourist

3 ~ 위로 •   **ⓒ** vehicle   **8** 다리 •   **ⓗ** landmark

4 ~뿐만 아니라 •   **ⓓ** over   **9** 가로질러 •   **ⓘ** bridge

5 차량 •   **ⓔ** another   **10** 관광객 •   **ⓙ** across

C 지문을 다시 읽으며 올바른 단어에 동그라미 하세요.

Bridges Around the World

People build bridges **1**(over / on) rivers, roads, and railroads. This way, people or **2**(ships / vehicles) can cross from one side to **3**(another / the other).

There are **4**(any / some) famous bridges. The Golden Gate Bridge is one of **5**(this / these) bridges. It is a landmark in San Francisco, California. Many tourists like to take pictures of it. Tower Bridge, in London, is **6**(another / the other) famous bridge in the world. It goes **7**(across / cross) the River Thames. In Australia, vehicles and trains as **8**(wall / well) as bicycles and pedestrians **9**(across / cross) the Sydney Harbor Bridge.

The world's **10**(largest / longest) bridge is the Danyang-Kunshan Grand Bridge in China. It opened in June 2011. It's almost 165 kilometers long. The **11**(oldest / newest) bridge is in Turkey. It **12**(built / was built) in 850 B.C., and it is still in use today.

Fun to Learn

A 우리말 뜻을 쓰고, 영단어를 세 번 쓰면서 철자를 익히세요.

1	brought	가져왔다	brought	brought	brought
2	board				
3	eel				
4	lobster				
5	shrimp				
6	clam				
7	jellyfish				
8	backwards				
9	electric				
10	identify				

B 우리말 뜻에 알맞은 영단어를 연결하세요.

1 새우 •　　　　　**ⓐ** electric

2 해파리 •　　　　**ⓑ** shrimp

3 가져왔다 •　　　**ⓒ** jellyfish

4 전기의 •　　　　**ⓓ** brought

5 바닷가재 •　　　**ⓔ** lobster

6 알아보다 •　　　**ⓕ** eel

7 장어 •　　　　　**ⓖ** backwards

8 뒤로 •　　　　　**ⓗ** identify

9 칠판, 판자 •　　　**ⓘ** board

10 조개 •　　　　**ⓙ** clam

C 지문을 다시 읽으며 올바른 단어에 동그라미 하세요.

Fun to Learn

Our teacher, Mr. Watson, **1**(bringed / brought) many pictures of sea animals to class. He put the pictures on the **2**(floor / board) and started to **3**(call / name) them. An eel, cuttlefish, lobster, shrimp, clam, jellyfish, swordfish, seahorse, whale, sea lion, and so **4**(in / on). We knew some of their names, but it was hard to **5**(draw / remember) all of them.

Mr. Watson told our class **6**(fun / boring) facts about each sea animal. Giant cuttlefish have green **7**(eyes / blood). Lobsters have blue blood and they live **8**(on to / up to) 100 years. Shrimps can only swim **9**(backwards / forwards). Electric eels can **10**(turn / light) up ten electric bulbs.

These fun facts let us **11**(identify / to identify) the animals easily. They were also fun to **12**(learn / name)!

A　우리말 뜻을 쓰고, 영단어를 세 번 쓰면서 철자를 익히세요.

1	produce	제작하다	produce	produce	produce
2	adventure				
3	film				
4	contain				
5	active				
6	fantastic				
7	audience				
8	imagination				
9	curiosity				
10	dream				

B　우리말 뜻에 알맞은 영단어를 연결하세요.

1 제작하다　　　●　　　**ⓐ** produce

2 꿈; 꿈을 꾸다　●　　　**ⓑ** film

3 모험　　　　　●　　　**ⓒ** curiosity

4 호기심　　　　●　　　**ⓓ** dream

5 영화; 촬영하다 ●　　　**ⓔ** adventure

6 담고 있다　　　●　　　**ⓕ** imagination

7 상상　　　　　●　　　**ⓖ** active

8 활동적인　　　●　　　**ⓗ** contain

9 관중, 청중　　●　　　**ⓘ** audience

10 환상적인　　　●　　　**ⓙ** fantastic

C 지문을 다시 읽으며 올바른 단어에 동그라미 하세요.

A Legendary Filmmaker

Have you **1**(see / seen) the movies *Jaws*, *E.T.*, and *Jurassic Park*? Steven Spielberg directed **2**(some / all) of these movies. He produced **3**(much / many) of the biggest Hollywood blockbusters **4**(on /over) the last 40 years. He used various themes and genres such as science **5**(fiction / nonfiction), humanism, and adventure in his films. Spielberg's films **6**(contained / directed) active and fantastic scenes. Audiences were very **7**(impress / impressed) with his movies and had fun **8**(watch / watching) them.

Steven Spielberg was born in Ohio, USA in 1946. From a young age, he had a big **9**(imagine / imagination) and was full of **10**(curious / curiosity). He filmed his first movie **11**(in / at) the age of twelve. It was a hit with his family and friends. These days, Spielberg still works hard to make great movies. He loves his job, and said, "I dream for a **12**(live / living)."

The Sword in the Stone

A 우리말 뜻을 쓰고, 영단어를 세 번 쓰면서 철자를 익히세요.

1 sword	검	sword	sword	sword
2 stone				
3 knight				
4 pull				
5 country				
6 fought				
7 fight				
8 crowd				
9 gather				
10 crown				

B 우리말 뜻에 알맞은 영단어를 연결하세요.

1 나라 ●	ⓐ sword		6 왕위에 앉히다 ●	ⓕ knight
2 검 ●	ⓑ gather		7 돌 ●	ⓖ fight
3 군중 ●	ⓒ crowd		8 (중세의) 기사 ●	ⓗ crown
4 싸웠다 ●	ⓓ country		9 뽑다, 당기다 ●	ⓘ stone
5 모이다 ●	ⓔ fought		10 싸우다 ●	ⓙ pull

C 지문을 다시 읽으며 올바른 단어에 동그라미 하세요.

The Sword in the Stone

There was a **1**(knife / sword) in a large stone. These words were on the stone: "ONLY THE **2**(KING / KNIGHT) CAN TAKE THE SWORD FROM THE STONE." Every knight tried to **3**(push / pull) the sword out of the stone. They pulled and pulled, but **4**(somebody / nobody) could pull it out of the stone.

There was a big **5**(war / tournament) in the country. Many knights came and **6**(fought / fight) on horses with swords in their hands. Arthur, a 15-year-old boy, wanted to fight with the other **7**(nights / knights), too. But he didn't have a sword.

Arthur went to the stone. He **8**(taked / took) the sword in his hand and pulled. It came out of the stone **9**(easy / easily). There was a **10**(crown / crowd) gathered around Arthur. The crowd cheered, and Arthur was **11**(crowded / crowned) King of England.

Rovers on Mars

A 우리말 뜻을 쓰고, 영단어를 세 번 쓰면서 철자를 익히세요.

1 develop	개발하다	develop	develop	develop
2 explore				
3 surface				
4 collect				
5 scientific				
6 sign				
7 ancient				
8 might				
9 useful				
10 tool				

B 우리말 뜻에 알맞은 영단어를 연결하세요.

1 유용한 • **ⓐ** life

2 인간 • **ⓑ** search

3 생명체 • **ⓒ** useful

4 신호, 징후 • **ⓓ** human

5 찾다, 살펴보다 • **ⓔ** sign

6 고대의 • **ⓕ** surface

7 탐험하다 • **ⓖ** scientific

8 과학적인 • **ⓗ** ancient

9 ~할지도 모른다 • **ⓘ** explore

10 표면 • **ⓙ** might

C 지문을 다시 읽으며 올바른 단어에 동그라미 하세요.

Rovers on Mars

Can people **1**(life / live) on Mars? Maybe **2**(someday / everyday). Rovers are robots developed **3**(by / with) NASA. These robots explore the surface of Mars and **4**(make / collect) scientific data. Rovers help us learn about Mars. They are like robot scientists.

Rovers study rocks and soil to **5**(teach / find) signs of ancient life. They also check the weather **6**(on / in) Mars. This is important for future trips **7**(when / where) people might go to Mars. Rovers help us learn **8**(as / if) Mars is safe for humans. Rovers search for useful things **9**(like / such) water. They help scientists make safe homes and tools for people. **10**(Knowing / Know) more about Mars makes it **11**(harder / easier) for people to live there.

Thanks **12**(for / to) rovers, the dream of living on Mars could come true one day!

My Uncle's Orchard

A 우리말 뜻을 쓰고, 영단어를 세 번 쓰면서 철자를 익히세요.

1 uncle	삼촌	uncle	uncle	uncle
2 orchard				
3 kind				
4 seed				
5 wonder				
6 pick up				
7 held				
8 flat				
9 oval				
10 coin				

B 우리말 뜻에 알맞은 영단어를 연결하세요.

1 과수원 ●	❶ uncle	**6** (손에) 들었다 ●
2 집어 들다 ●	❷ coin	**7** 타원형 ●
3 삼촌 ●	❸ kind	**8** 납작한 ●
4 동전 ●	❹ orchard	**9** 궁금해하다 ●
5 종류 ●	❺ pick up	**10** 씨앗 ●

6 (손에) 들었다 ● ❻ oval
7 타원형 ● ❼ seed
8 납작한 ● ❽ wonder
9 궁금해하다 ● ❾ held
10 씨앗 ● ❿ flat

C 지문을 다시 읽으며 올바른 단어에 동그라미 하세요.

My Uncle's Orchard

Jerry visited his uncle's **1**(farm / orchard). There **2**(was / were) a lot of different kinds of fruit trees. He also found many fruit **3**(seeds / flowers) on the ground. They all had **4**(same / different) sizes, shapes, and colors. Jerry wondered what **5**(shape / kind) of seeds they were, so he asked his uncle.

He **6**(pulled / picked) up a seed which was **7**(as / so) big as a ping-pong ball. It was brown and **8**(around / round). His uncle said that it was an avocado seed. Then Jerry **9**(hold / held) a flat and oval-shaped seed that was the **10**(color / size) of a coin. That was an apricot seed.

He found a seed that he knew. It was the seed of his **11**(favorite / best) fruit. It looked **12**(as / like) a pea and it was beige. Yes! It was a cherry seed.

A 우리말 뜻을 쓰고, 영단어를 세 번 쓰면서 철자를 익히세요.

1	celebrate	기념하다	celebrate	celebrate	celebrate
2	November				
3	harvest				
4	crop				
5	starve				
6	fail				
7	succeed				
8	invite				
9	successful				
10	pumpkin				

B 우리말 뜻에 알맞은 영단어를 연결하세요.

1 기념하다 ●	ⓐ celebrate	6 실패하다　●	ⓕ November
2 호박　●	ⓑ crop	7 11월　●	ⓖ harvest
3 성공하다 ●	ⓒ invite	8 수확하다 ●	ⓗ fail
4 초대하다 ●	ⓓ succeed	9 굶주리다 ●	ⓘ successful
5 농작물　●	ⓔ pumpkin	10 성공적인 ●	ⓙ starve

C 지문을 다시 읽으며 올바른 단어에 동그라미 하세요.

Thanksgiving Day

Thanksgiving Day is celebrated **1**(in / on) the fourth Thursday in November in the USA. It **2**(celebrates / is celebrated) as a day of harvesting crops.

In the winter of 1620, **3**(all / half) of the English people **4**(know / known) as Pilgrims starved to **5**(die / death) because they **6**(failed / had failed) to harvest crops in the USA. Native Americans taught the Pilgrims **7**(what / how) to grow and harvest crops. The next year, in 1621, the Pilgrims **8**(succeeded / successful) in harvesting crops.

The Pilgrims invited the Native Americans to celebrate the **9**(succeeded / successful) harvest. The Pilgrims and the Native Americans **10**(eat / ate) corn, beans, and pumpkins. They also caught **11**(fishes / fish) and ate them together. This is **12**(how / why) Americans celebrate Thanksgiving Day.

Cupid

A 우리말 뜻을 쓰고, 영단어를 세 번 쓰면서 철자를 익히세요.

1 Roman	로마의	Roman	Roman	Roman
2 god				
3 Greek				
4 goddess				
5 beauty				
6 myth				
7 arrow				
8 bow				
9 shot				
10 shoot				

B 우리말 뜻에 알맞은 영단어를 연결하세요.

1 그리스어 ●   ⓐ beauty

2 로마의 ●   ⓑ arrow

3 쏘다 ●   ⓒ Greek

4 화살 ●   ⓓ shoot

5 아름다움 ●   ⓔ Roman

6 여신 ●   ⓕ shot

7 쐈다 ●   ⓖ goddess

8 신 ●   ⓗ myth

9 신화 ●   ⓘ god

10 활 ●   ⓙ bow

C 지문을 다시 읽으며 올바른 단어에 동그라미 하세요.

Cupid

Cupid was the Roman **1**(god / goddess) of love. He was also called Eros in **2**(Roman / Greek). He was the son of Venus, the **3**(god / goddess) of love and beauty.

There are **4**(myths / mythes) about Cupid and his arrows. Cupid's arrows could make you fall in love. Cupid had wings on his **5**(arms / back), so he could fly. He carried a bow and two types of arrows. One had a **6**(sharp / blunt) golden point, and the other had a **7**(sharp / blunt) lead point.

When Cupid shot a person with the **8**(golden / lead) arrow, this person fell in love with the **9**(so / very) next person he or she saw. But when Cupid shot someone with the **10**(golden / lead) arrow, this person **11**(killed / hated) the next person he or she saw.

So watch out! Cupid **12**(will / might) shoot you someday.

A　우리말 뜻을 쓰고, 영단어를 세 번 쓰면서 철자를 익히세요.

1	spend	(시간을) 보내다	spend	spend	spend
2	entire				
3	species				
4	human				
5	lung				
6	gill				
7	eyelid				
8	always				
9	exception				
10	shark				

B　우리말 뜻에 알맞은 영단어를 연결하세요.

1 허파　　　•　　　ⓐ human
2 인간, 사람　•　　　ⓑ spend
3 전체의　　•　　　ⓒ always
4 (시간을) 보내다 •　ⓓ lung
5 항상　　　•　　　ⓔ entire

6 (생물) 종　•　　　ⓕ gill
7 눈꺼풀　　•　　　ⓖ shark
8 아가미　　•　　　ⓗ species
9 상어　　　•　　　ⓘ exception
10 예외　　　•　　　ⓙ eyelid

C 지문을 다시 읽으며 올바른 단어에 동그라미 하세요.

All About Fish

Fish spend their entire **1**(lifes / lives) in water. There are 32,000 different **2**(species / specials) of fish. Some **3**(fish / fishes) are up to 2,700 centimeters long and **4**(other / others) are only 8 millimeters long.

Fish need oxygen to live, just like humans. Humans have **5**(lungs / gills) to breathe air, but fish have **6**(lungs / gills). Gills help fish **7**(breath / breathe) under water.

8(Like / Unlike) humans, fish also sleep. They sleep **9**(by / with) their eyes open because they don't have **10**(eyelashes / eyelids). But there are always exceptions. Some sharks have eyelids. But they sleep with their eyes **11**(open / close). If you see a fish moving slowly, it might be sleeping. Most fish move when they're sleeping **12**(why / because) they need to breathe oxygen.

Jenny's Closet

A 우리말 뜻을 쓰고, 영단어를 세 번 쓰면서 철자를 익히세요.

1 messy	지저분한	messy	messy	messy
2 closet				
3 stuff				
4 bent				
5 finally				
6 piece				
7 back				
8 bury				
9 rip				
10 from now on				

B 우리말 뜻에 알맞은 영단어를 연결하세요.

1 일부, 부품 ●	ⓐ stuff	**6** 굽혔다 ●	ⓕ finally
2 묻다 ●	ⓑ messy	**7** 뒤쪽 ●	ⓖ bent
3 지저분한 ●	ⓒ piece	**8** 마침내 ●	ⓗ closet
4 앞으로는 ●	ⓓ bury	**9** 찢다 ●	ⓘ back
5 물건 ●	ⓔ from now on	**10** 옷장 ●	ⓙ rip

Water, Wind, and Ice

C 지문을 다시 읽으며 올바른 단어에 동그라미 하세요.

Jenny's Closet

Jenny had a big **1**(clean / messy) closet in her room. She liked to put all her **2**(stuff / staff) in the closet. She put her clothes, caps, socks, bags, dolls, hair pins, and **3**(still / even) shoes in it. Her mother always told her to clean **4**(out / over) the closet. But Jenny liked it that way.

One day, Jenny **5**(invited / was invited) to a friend's birthday party. She wanted to wear her purple shirt, but she couldn't find it. Jenny **6**(bend / bent) over and finally found a piece of the shirt at the **7**(front / back) of the closet. She pulled it **8**(hard / hardly). Suddenly, everything came out with the shirt. Jenny was **9**(buryed / buried) under her stuff, and her purple shirt was **10**(riped / ripped).

"From now **11**(in / on), I'll **12**(ever / never) have a messy closet again."

Water, Wind, and Ice

A   우리말 뜻을 쓰고, 영단어를 세 번 쓰면서 철자를 익히세요.

1	erosion	침식	erosion	erosion	erosion
2	surface				
3	peak				
4	valley				
5	coastline				
6	muddy				
7	rainstorm				
8	landscape				
9	area				
10	pebble				

B   우리말 뜻에 알맞은 영단어를 연결하세요.

1 풍경 ●	ⓐ landscape	**6** 계곡 ●	ⓕ erosion
2 표면 ●	ⓑ peak	**7** 진흙투성이인 ●	ⓖ valley
3 해안선 ●	ⓒ surface	**8** 침식 ●	ⓗ muddy
4 지역 ●	ⓓ area	**9** 폭풍우 ●	ⓘ pebble
5 산꼭대기 ●	ⓔ coastline	**10** 자갈 ●	ⓙ rainstorm

C 지문을 다시 읽으며 올바른 단어에 동그라미 하세요.

Water, Wind, and Ice

Water, wind, and ice **1**(wear / pick) away the land. This **2**(calls / is called) erosion. Erosion is the **3**(sign / removal) of rocks and soil **4**(with / by) wind, water, ice, and gravity. Erosion **5**(causes / changes) the earth's surface. This can change mountain **6**(peaks / picks), valleys, and coastlines. Erosion can happen **7**(slowly / quickly) or take thousands of years.

Do you know why streams and lakes get **8**(dry / muddy) after a rainstorm? It is a **9**(sign / removal) that erosion is taking place. Rainstorms change the landscape.

Wind **10**(causes / changes) erosion, especially in dry areas. Wind picks up and carries **11**(on / away) sand, light rocks, and pebbles. Wind changes the landscape, too. Ice causes erosion in cold areas. Giant rivers of ice, called **12**(glaciers / glasses), move slowly and change the valleys and mountains.

The Little Match Girl

A 우리말 뜻을 쓰고, 영단어를 세 번 쓰면서 철자를 익히세요.

1 match	성냥	match	match	match
2 lean				
3 against				
4 wall				
5 lit				
6 stove				
7 went out				
8 gone				
9 struck				
10 continuously				

B 우리말 뜻에 알맞은 영단어를 연결하세요.

1 성냥 •   ⓐ continuously   **6** 난로 •   ⓕ against

2 기대다 •   ⓑ gone   **7** (성냥을) 그었다 •   ⓖ stove

3 불을 붙였다 •   ⓒ lit   **8** 담, 벽 •   ⓗ wall

4 계속해서 •   ⓓ lean   **9** (불이) 꺼졌다 •   ⓘ went out

5 사라진, 떠난 •   ⓔ match   **10** ~에 대고 •   ⓙ struck

C 지문을 다시 읽으며 올바른 단어에 동그라미 하세요.

The Little Match Girl

It was a very cold night. The little match girl was leaning **1**(again / against) a wall outside a house. She **2**(isn't / wasn't) wearing a coat or shoes. She was so cold. She **3**(lighted / lit) a match to warm **4**(her / herself).

The little match girl **5**(held / holded) the match, and she could see a warm stove in the light. Her feet **6**(was / were) warm. But when the match went out, the stove was **7**(go / gone). She **8**(striked / struck) another match. She could see a **9**(stove / table) full of delicious food and a Christmas tree. But the match went **10**(away / out) again.

She **11**(continue / continuously) lit her matches. This time she could see her dead grandmother, who loved her so much. She wanted to **12**(follow / lean) her grandmother.

3D Printers

A 우리말 뜻을 쓰고, 영단어를 세 번 쓰면서 철자를 익히세요.

1 text	글자	text	text	text
2 real				
3 squeeze				
4 material				
5 plastic				
6 metal				
7 rubber				
8 object				
9 individual				
10 technology				

B 우리말 뜻에 알맞은 영단어를 연결하세요.

1 고무 •	ⓐ individual	**6** 기술 •	ⓕ real
2 플라스틱 •	ⓑ rubber	**7** 금속 •	ⓖ text
3 짜내다 •	ⓒ object	**8** 실제의 •	ⓗ technology
4 개인 •	ⓓ plastic	**9** 글자 •	ⓘ material
5 물체 •	ⓔ squeeze	**10** 재료 •	ⓙ metal

C 지문을 다시 읽으며 올바른 단어에 동그라미 하세요.

3D Printers

A 3D printer isn't like a **1**(special / regular) printer. Instead of printing simple text on a single piece of paper, a 3D printer can print a **2**(real / really) thing! 3D printers spray or squeeze raw **3**(materials / objects) like plastic, metal, paper, rubber, silicon, or any other kind of material which **4**(needs / is needed) to print **5**(in / out) the things. Three-dimensional **6**(materials / objects) such as musical instruments, human body parts, shoes, cars, and even a house can be **7**(make / made) with 3D printers.

There are many different kinds of 3D printers **8**(these / those) days. Unfortunately, they are still too **9**(bright / expensive) for most **10**(individuals / groups) to buy and use at home. **11**(However / Whatever), with 3D printers creating everything from clothing to body parts, the future appears **12**(bright / expensive) for 3D printing technology.

What Happens at City Hall?

A 우리말 뜻을 쓰고, 영단어를 세 번 쓰면서 철자를 익히세요.

1	newspaper	신문	newspaper	newspaper	newspaper
2	reporter				
3	interview				
4	mayor				
5	office				
6	lead				
7	meeting				
8	regularly				
9	decision				
10	example				

B 우리말 뜻에 알맞은 영단어를 연결하세요.

1 기자 •	**ⓐ** lead		6 회의 •	**ⓕ** office
2 결정 •	**ⓑ** mayor		7 인터뷰하다 •	**ⓖ** example
3 신문 •	**ⓒ** reporter		8 사무실 •	**ⓗ** regularly
4 이끌다 •	**ⓓ** newspaper		9 정기적으로 •	**ⓘ** interview
5 시장 •	**ⓔ** decision		10 예 •	**ⓙ** meeting

The Earth Is Spinning

C 지문을 다시 읽으며 올바른 단어에 동그라미 하세요.

What Happens at City Hall?

Stacy is a school newspaper **1**(mayor / reporter). She wanted to write an article about City Hall. She thought, "Everyone **2**(know / knows) where City Hall is. But do we know what **3**(allows / happens) there?"

A few days later, Stacy interviewed the **4**(mayor / reporter), Janet Duncan. The mayor's office was in City Hall.

"What do you do here?" asked Stacy.

"As the mayor, I **5**(lead / imagine) the city council meetings," said Janet. "We meet **6**(regular / regularly) to make important **7**(examples / decisions) for our town."

"Can you give me an **8**(example / decision)?" asked Stacy.

"Well, **9**(lead / imagine) someone wants to open a big department store right next to an elementary school. It could be dangerous **10**(before / because) many shoppers would drive near the school. So, we would not **11**(allow / happen) that."

"Oh, so you keep our town **12**(safe / safety)!" said Stacy.

The Earth Is Spinning

A 우리말 뜻을 쓰고, 영단어를 세 번 쓰면서 철자를 익히세요.

1	below	아래에	below	below	below
2	spin				
3	marble				
4	smooth				
5	movement				
6	seem				
7	rise				
8	set				
9	toward				
10	complete				

B 우리말 뜻에 알맞은 영단어를 연결하세요.

1 완료하다 •　　　　•ⓐ rise　　　　**6** ~쪽으로 •　　　　•ⓕ seem

2 돌다; 회전 •　　　　•ⓑ marble　　　　**7** 매끄러운 •　　　　•ⓖ set

3 아래에 •　　　　•ⓒ complete　　　　**8** (해가) 지다 •　　　　•ⓗ smooth

4 (해가) 뜨다 •　　　　•ⓓ spin　　　　**9** ~인 것 같다 •　　　　•ⓘ movement

5 구슬 •　　　　•ⓔ below　　　　**10** 움직임 •　　　　•ⓙ toward

C 지문을 다시 읽으며 올바른 단어에 동그라미 하세요.

The Earth Is Spinning

Did you know that you are moving right now? That's right! In Korea, the ground **1**(above / below) you is moving at almost 1,300 kilometers per **2**(hour / minute)! And it's taking you with it!

The earth is **3**(spining / spinning). Put a marble on a smooth table. Spin it. That's **4**(why / what) the earth is doing. Of course, we don't feel this **5**(moving / movement). To us, it **6**(seem / seems) like the sun is moving. That's **7**(why / what) we say the sun "rises" in the morning and **8**("puts" / "sets") at night. Actually, the sun doesn't move.

As our side of the earth moves toward the sun, we have **9**(daytime / night). When it moves away, we have **10**(daytime / night). The earth **11**(moves / takes) 24 hours to complete one **12**(movement / spin). That's why one day is 24 hours long!

Robin Hood

A 우리말 뜻을 쓰고, 영단어를 세 번 쓰면서 철자를 익히세요.

1 rob	도둑질하다	rob	rob	rob
2 go through				
3 attack				
4 sheriff				
5 catch				
6 plan				
7 competition				
8 choose				
9 prize				
10 hit				

B 우리말 뜻에 알맞은 영단어를 연결하세요.

1 공격하다 •　　　　**ⓐ** go through　　　　**6** 도둑질하다 •　　　　**ⓕ** choose

2 맞혔다 •　　　　**ⓑ** catch　　　　**7** 계획 •　　　　**ⓖ** plan

3 통과하다 •　　　　**ⓒ** sheriff　　　　**8** 선택하다 •　　　　**ⓗ** rob

4 잡다 •　　　　**ⓓ** hit　　　　**9** 상, 상품 •　　　　**ⓘ** competition

5 주 장관 •　　　　**ⓔ** attack　　　　**10** 대회 •　　　　**ⓙ** prize

C 지문을 다시 읽으며 올바른 단어에 동그라미 하세요.

Robin Hood

Robin Hood was a man **1**(who / which) lived in Sherwood Forest in England. He **2**(robed / robbed) the rich and gave to **3**(a / the) poor. That made the **4**(poor / rich) scared of going through Sherwood Forest. They knew Robin Hood would **5**(attack / choose) them.

One day, the **6**(sheriff / archer) wanted to catch Robin Hood, so he made a plan. He held a competition to choose the best **7**(sheriff / archer) in town. The sheriff knew that Robin Hood would come to the **8**(forest / competition) because he was a good archer.

A man in green clothes was the **9**(first / last) person to shoot for the **10**(last / first) prize. The arrow went **11**(to / through) the bullseye, and another two arrows **12**(hit / hitted) the sheriff's chair. It was Robin Hood.

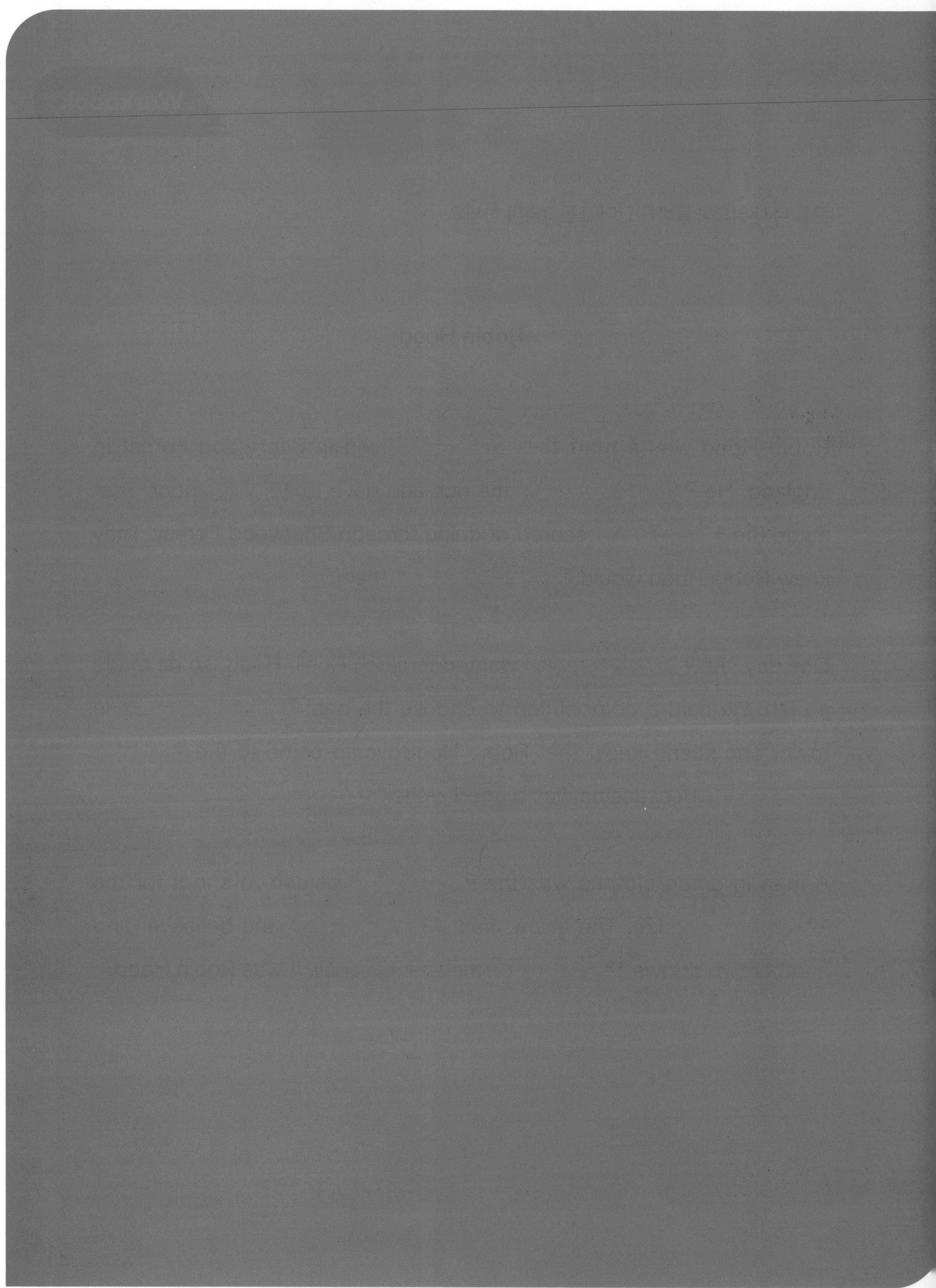

기적의 직독직해

120 words A

Answers

동물들은 그들의 꼬리를 많은 다양한 방법으로 사용해요. 원숭이 같은 어떤 동물들은 나무에서 나무로 휙 이동하기 위해 꼬리를 사용해요. 도마뱀 같은 어떤 동물들은 자기 방어를 위해 꼬리를 사용해요. 전갈은 꼬리를 무기로 사용해요. 그 안에는 독이 있어요. 물고기는 물을 헤치며 이동하기 위해 꼬리를 사용해요. 캥거루와 다람쥐는 자신이 균형을 잡는 데 도움을 주기 위해 꼬리를 사용해요. 새들은 자신이 하늘을 나는 데 도움을 주기 위해 꼬리를 사용해요.

고양이와 개는 의사소통을 하기 위해 꼬리를 사용해요. 그들은 두려움과 흥분 같은 많은 감정들을 표현하기 위해 꼬리를 사용할 수 있어요. 개는 그들의 주인을 반기기 위해 꼬리를 흔들어요.

여러분은 꼬리를 가진 애완동물을 가지고 있나요? 그 애완동물은 꼬리를 어떻게 사용하나요?

Comprehension Check · 13쪽

A 1. F 원숭이는 자기 방어를 위해 꼬리를 사용해요.
    2. T 전갈은 꼬리를 무기로 사용해요.
    3. T 개는 의사소통을 하기 위해 꼬리를 사용해요.

B 1. ⓑ 이 지문은 주로 <u>동물들의 꼬리</u>에 대한 거예요.
      ⓐ 동물들의 무기들 ⓒ 동물들의 의사소통
    2. ⓒ 어떤 동물이 꼬리를 이용해서 물을 헤치며 이동하나요?
      ⓐ 캥거루 ⓑ 다람쥐 ⓒ 물고기
    3. ⓐ 개들은 왜 꼬리를 흔드나요?
      ⓐ 그들의 주인을 반기기 위해서
      ⓑ 나무에서 나무로 휙 이동하기 위해서
      ⓒ 그들 스스로 균형을 잡기 위해서

C 1. self-defense 도마뱀 같은 어떤 동물들은 <u>자기 방어</u>를 위해 꼬리를 사용해요.
    2. weapon 전갈은 꼬리를 <u>무기</u>로 사용해요.
    3. communicate 고양이와 개는 <u>의사소통</u>을 하기 위해 꼬리를 사용해요.

Read and Understand · 14쪽

1. 많은 다양한 방법으로
2. 휙 이동하기 위해
3. 자기 방어를 위해

4. 무기로
5. 그것은 독을 갖고 있다
6. 물을 헤치며 이동하기 위해
7. 그들 자신이 균형 잡는 데 도움을 주기 위해
8. 그들 자신이 나는 데 도움을 주기 위해
9. 의사소통을 하기 위해
10. 두려움과 흥분 같은
11. 그들의 주인을 반기기 위해
12. 꼬리를 가진 애완동물을
13. 그것의 꼬리를

Grammar Point · 15쪽

1. 우리는 너를 만나기 위해 여기에 왔다.
2. 나는 공부하기 위해 도서관에 갔다.

Workbook

A
1. 휙 움직이다
2. 도마뱀
3. 무기
4. 독
5. 균형을 잡다
6. 의사소통을 하다
7. 표현하다
8. 감정
9. 두려움
10. 주인

B
1. ⓒ
2. ⓔ
3. ⓐ
4. ⓑ
5. ⓓ
6. ⓖ
7. ⓗ
8. ⓕ
9. ⓙ
10. ⓘ

C
1. their
2. swing
3. lizards
4. weapon
5. poison
6. balance
7. fly
8. communicate
9. express
10. excitement
11. greet
12. with

어제 아침에 알포는 먹지도 움직이지도 않았어요. 그는 콧물이 나고 기침도 했어요. 아빠와 나는 알포를 동물 병원에 데려갔어요. 수의사 선생님은 알포가 독감에 걸렸다고 말씀하셨어요. 또, 알포를 실내에 있게 하고 며칠 동안 약을 주라고 말씀하셨어요. 아빠는 내가 알포의 형이므로, 알포를 잘 돌보는 것은 나의 일이라고 말씀하셨어요.

집으로 돌아와서, 나는 알포 밑에 깨끗한 담요를 깔아 줬어요. 알포에게 물과 약도 줬어요. 규칙적으로 먹이도 줬어요. 나는 알포를 따뜻하게 유지해 줬어요. 나는 하루 종일 알포를 돌봤어요. 나는 알포의 집 옆에서 잠이 들었어요.

오늘 아침, 축축한 뭔가가 나를 깨웠어요. 그것은 알포였어요! 알포는 무척 좋아 보였어요! 사랑해, 알포야!

Comprehension Check 17쪽

A 1. T 알포는 독감에 걸렸기 때문에 아팠어요.
2. T 소년은 하루 종일 알포를 돌봤어요.
3. F 알포는 나에게 물과 약을 줬어요.

B 1. ⓐ 이 지문은 주로 소년과 그의 개에 대한 거예요.
ⓑ 소년과 그의 아빠 ⓒ 동물 병원
2. ⓑ 소년은 집으로 돌아와서 알포 밑에 무엇을 깔아 줬나요?
ⓐ 젖은 수건 ⓑ 깨끗한 담요 ⓒ 약
3. ⓑ 소년이 하루 종일 알포를 돌본 후에, 어떤 일이 일어났나요?
ⓐ 소년은 그의 형을 만났어요.
ⓑ 소년은 알포의 집 옆에서 잠이 들었어요.
ⓒ 소년은 약을 먹었어요.

C 1. runny, cough 알포는 콧물이 나고 기침도 했어요.
2. job, care 아빠는 내가 알포의 형이므로, 알포를 잘 돌보는 것은 나의 일이라고 말씀하셨어요.
3. wet 오늘 아침, 축축한 뭔가가 나를 깨웠어요.

Read and Understand 18쪽

1. 알포는 먹지도 움직이지도 않았다
2. 콧물과 기침을
3. 알포를 데려갔다
4. 그가 독감에 걸렸다고
5. 그리고 그에게 약을 주라고
6. 그를 잘 돌보는 것은
7. 나는 깨끗한 담요를 깔아 줬다
8. 나는 그에게 줬다
9. 나를 그를 따뜻하게 유지해 줬다
10. 하루 종일
11. 나는 잠이 들었다
12. 축축한 뭔가가
13. 알포는 무척 좋아 보였다

Grammar Point 19쪽

1. 나는 돈이 없기 때문에 컵을 살 수 없다.
2. 우리는 학생이기 때문에 열심히 공부해야 한다.

Workbook

A
1. 콧물
2. 기침
3. 수의사
4. 독감
5. 약
6. ~를 돌보다
7. 담요
8. 먹이를 줬다
9. 젖은
10. 옆에

B
1. ⓓ
2. ⓔ
3. ⓑ
4. ⓐ
5. ⓒ
6. ⓗ
7. ⓕ
8. ⓖ
9. ⓙ
10. ⓘ

C
1. didn't
2. runny
3. took
4. flu
5. inside
6. medicine
7. since
8. blanket
9. fed
10. after
11. asleep
12. something wet

1845년에 플로렌스 나이팅게일은 영국에서 간호사가 됐어요. 몇 년 후, 나이팅게일은 크림 전쟁에서 병들고 부상당한 군인들의 열악한 치료에 대해 읽었어요. 그녀는 크림 반도로 가서 더럽고 붐비는 병원들을 발견했어요. 그녀는 더 많은 군인들이 전쟁에서의 부상보다 질병으로 인해 죽는다는 것을 알았어요.

나이팅게일은 병원을 청소하고 부상당한 군인들을 돌보기 위해 열심히 일했어요. 플로렌스는 저녁마다 램프를 들고 부상당한 군인들을 확인하며 병원을 돌아다녔어요. 이런 이유로 많은 군인들은 그녀를 "램프를 든 여인"이라고 불렀어요. 그녀 덕분에, 질병으로 죽는 군인들이 더 적어졌어요.

플로렌스는 간호사를 위한 나이팅게일 학교를 설립했어요. 그녀는 세상에서 가장 훌륭한 간호사였어요.

Comprehension Check · 21쪽

A 1. F 플로렌스 나이팅게일은 1845년에 태어났어요.
2. T 더 많은 군인들이 전쟁에서의 부상보다 질병으로 인해 죽었어요.
3. F 플로렌스는 군인들을 위한 나이팅게일 학교를 설립했어요.

B 1. ⓑ 이 지문은 주로 플로렌스 나이팅게일에 대한 거예요.
　ⓐ 크림 전쟁　ⓒ 질병들
2. ⓒ 플로렌스는 왜 크림 반도의 병원에서 열심히 일했나요?
　ⓐ 램프를 든 여인을 만나기 위해서
　ⓑ 간호사가 되기 위해서
　ⓒ 부상당한 군인들을 돌보기 위해서
3. ⓒ 군인들은 왜 플로렌스를 "램프를 든 여인"이라고 불렀나요?
　ⓐ 그녀가 간호사를 위한 학교를 설립했기 때문에
　ⓑ 그녀가 저녁마다 램프를 고쳤기 때문에
　ⓒ 그녀가 저녁마다 램프를 들고 부상당한 군인들을 확인했기 때문에

C 1. became 1845년에 플로렌스 나이팅게일은 영국에서 간호사가 됐어요.
2. poor, injured 몇 년 후, 나이팅게일은 크림 전쟁에서 병들고 부상당한 군인들의 열악한 치료에 대해 읽었어요.
3. carrying, checking 플로렌스는 저녁마다 램프를 들고 부상당한 군인들을 확인하며 병원을 돌아다녔어요.

Read and Understand · 22쪽

1. 간호사가 되었다
2. 열악한 치료에 대해
3. 더럽고 붐비는 병원들을
4. 전쟁에서의 부상으로 인한 것보다
5. 부상당한 군인들을
6. 램프를 들고
7. 이런 이유로
8. 더 적은 군인들이
9. 간호사들을 위한
10. 그녀는 최고의 간호사였다

Grammar Point · 23쪽

1. 선생님은 학생들을 확인하면서 교실을 둘러보았다.
2. 피터는 반바지만 입고서 아침마다 조깅을 했다.

Workbook

A
1. 영국
2. 치료
3. 부상당한
4. 군인
5. 붐비는
6. 부상, 상처
7. 램프
8. ~을 확인하다
9. 이유
10. 설립하다

B
1. ⓒ
2. ⓓ
3. ⓐ
4. ⓔ
5. ⓑ
6. ⓘ
7. ⓗ
8. ⓙ
9. ⓖ
10. ⓕ

C
1. In
2. became
3. read
4. injured
5. died
6. injuries
7. evenings
8. checking
9. For
10. Thanks
11. fewer
12. established

The Lion and the Mouse | 사자와 생쥐

작은 쥐 한 마리가 갈색 언덕을 오르기 시작하더니 미끄러져 내려왔어요. 하지만 그 언덕은 잠자는 사자의 등이었어요! 쥐한테 방해를 받아서 사자는 잠에서 깼어요. 화난 사자가 발톱 사이로 그 쥐를 잡았어요.

"제발 저를 놓아 주세요. 그러면 언젠가 다시 와서 당신을 도와줄게요." 쥐가 말했어요.

사자는 웃었어요. "넌 너무 작아! 작은 쥐가 어떻게 나를 도와주겠다는 거야?" 하지만 사자는 쥐 덕분에 웃을 수 있었기 때문에 그 작은 쥐를 놓아 줬어요.

다음 날, 사자는 덫에 걸렸어요. 쥐가 그에게 와서 이빨로 밧줄을 끊기 시작했어요. 마침내, 사자는 덫에서 빠져나올 수 있었어요.

"사랑하는 친구야, 결국 네가 나를 구했구나. 고마워." 사자가 말했어요.

"당신을 도울 수 있어서 기뻐요." 쥐가 말했어요.

Comprehension Check 25쪽

A 1. T 작은 쥐 한 마리가 사자 등에 올랐다가 미끄러져 내려왔어요.
2. T 사자는 발톱 사이로 쥐를 잡았어요.
3. F 사자는 덫에 걸린 쥐를 구해 줬어요.

B 1. ⓐ 이야기를 통해 무엇을 배울 수 있나요?
   ⓐ 모든 것이 어떤 식으로든 도움이 될 수 있다.
   ⓑ 한 가지 일만 잘하는 게 낫다.
   ⓒ 작은 친구들과 싸우면 안 된다.
2. ⓒ 사자가 쥐를 놓아준 다음 날, 사자에게 어떤 일이 일어났나요?
   ⓐ 그는 갈색 언덕을 올랐어요.
   ⓑ 그는 발톱 사이로 쥐를 잡았어요.
   ⓒ 그는 덫에 걸렸어요.
3. ⓒ 쥐는 어떻게 사자가 덫에서 나오도록 도왔나요?
   ⓐ 쥐는 그의 발로 밧줄을 끊었어요.
   ⓑ 쥐는 그의 꼬리로 밧줄을 끊었어요.
   ⓒ 쥐는 그의 이빨로 밧줄을 끊었어요.

C 1. climbing 작은 쥐 한 마리가 갈색 언덕을 오르기 시작하더니 미끄러져 내려왔어요.
2. Bothered 쥐한테 방해를 받아서 사자는 잠에서 깼어요.
3. let, laugh 하지만 사자는 쥐 덕분에 웃을 수 있었기 때문에 그 작은 쥐를 놓아 줬어요.

Read and Understand 26쪽

1. 오르기 시작했다
2. 잠자는 사자의 등
3. 사자는 잠에서 깼다
4. 그의 발톱 사이로
5. 제발 저를 놓아 주세요
6. 작은 쥐가 어떻게 나를 도울 수 있지?
7. 그 작은 쥐를 놓아 줬다
8. 사자는 잡혔다
9. 그의 이빨로
10. 사자는 나올 수 있었다
11. 네가 나를 구했구나
12. 제가 당신을 도울 수 있어서

Grammar Point 27쪽

1. 그는 샤워를 하기 시작했다.
2. 나는 노래를 부르기 시작했다.

Workbook

A
1. 시작했다
2. ~에 오르다
3. 방해하다
4. 잡았다
5. 발톱
6. 언젠가
7. 덫
8. 이빨들
9. 구하다
10. 결국

B
1. ⓒ
2. ⓑ
3. ⓓ
4. ⓐ
5. ⓔ
6. ⓖ
7. ⓗ
8. ⓕ
9. ⓙ
10. ⓘ

C
1. slid
2. sleeping
3. Bothered
4. between
5. let
6. go
7. thanks
8. was caught
9. began
10. teeth
11. after
12. glad

사람들은 강, 도로, 철로 위에 다리를 지어요. 이 방법으로, 사람들이나 차들은 한쪽에서 다른 쪽으로 건너갈 수 있어요.

몇 개의 유명한 다리들이 있어요. 금문교는 이러한 다리들 중 하나예요. 그것은 캘리포니아 샌프란시스코에 있는 랜드마크예요. 많은 관광객들이 그것의 사진을 찍는 것을 좋아해요. 런던에 있는 타워 브리지는 세계에서 또 다른 유명한 다리예요. 그것은 템스 강을 가로질러요. 호주에서는 자전거들과 보행자들뿐만 아니라 차들과 기차들도 시드니 하버 브리지를 건너요.

세계에서 가장 긴 다리는 중국에 있는 단양-쿤샨 대교예요. 이 다리는 2011년 6월에 개통됐어요. 이 다리는 길이가 거의 165킬로미터예요. 가장 오래된 다리는 터키에 있어요. 이 다리는 기원전 850년에 지어졌고, 오늘날에도 여전히 사용되고 있어요.

Comprehension Check   29쪽

A 1. F 사람들은 집들과 건물들 위에 다리를 지어요.
   2. T 금문교는 유명한 다리예요.
   3. F 세계에서 가장 긴 다리는 타워 브리지예요.

B 1. ⓑ 이 지문은 주로 세계의 다리들에 대한 거예요.
      ⓐ 미국의 다리들 ⓒ 긴 다리들
   2. ⓒ 사람들은 한쪽에서 다른 쪽으로 건너가기 위해 강 위에 무엇을 짓나요?
      ⓐ 철길 ⓑ 교통수단들 ⓒ 다리
   3. ⓑ 오늘날에도 여전히 사용되고 있는 가장 오래된 다리는 어디에 있나요?
      ⓐ 미국에 ⓑ 터키에 ⓒ 중국에

C 1. side 이 방법으로, 사람들이나 차들은 한쪽에서 다른 쪽으로 건너갈 수 있어요.
   2. well, pedestrians 호주에서는 자전거들과 보행자들뿐만 아니라 차들과 기차들도 시드니 하버 브리지를 건너요.
   3. longest 세계에서 가장 긴 다리는 중국에 있는 단양-쿤샨 대교예요.

Read and Understand   30쪽

1. 사람들은 다리를 짓는다
2. 한쪽에서 다른 쪽으로
3. 몇 개의 유명한 다리들이
4. 이 다리들 중 하나이다
5. 그것은 랜드마크이다
6. 사진을 찍는 것을
7. 또 다른 유명한 다리이다
8. 그것은 가로지른다
9. 자전거들과 보행자들뿐만 아니라
10. 세계에서 가장 긴 다리는
11. 2011년 6월에
12. 그것은 길이가 거의 165킬로미터이다
13. 가장 오래된 다리는
14. 그것은 지어졌다

Grammar Point   31쪽

1. 나는 영어뿐만 아니라 중국어도 배우고 싶다.
2. 그 트럭은 바위뿐만 아니라 흙도 나른다.

Workbook

A
1. 다리
2. ~ 위로
3. 철로
4. 차량
5. 건너다
6. 랜드마크
7. 관광객
8. 또 다른
9. 가로질러
10. ~뿐만 아니라

B
1. ⓔ
2. ⓑ
3. ⓓ
4. ⓐ
5. ⓒ
6. ⓗ
7. ⓕ
8. ⓘ
9. ⓙ
10. ⓖ

C
1. over
2. vehicles
3. the other
4. some
5. these
6. another
7. across
8. well
9. cross
10. longest
11. oldest
12. was built

우리의 왓슨 선생님은 많은 바다 동물들의 사진들을 수업에 가져 오셨어요. 그는 그 사진들을 칠판에 붙이고 그것들의 이름을 말하기 시작했어요. 장어, 갑오징어, 바닷가재, 새우, 조개, 해파리, 황새치, 해마, 고래, 바다사자 등등. 우리는 그것들의 이름 중 몇 개는 알았지만, 그것들 모두를 기억하는 것은 어려웠어요.

왓슨 선생님은 우리 반에게 각각의 바다 동물에 대한 재미있는 사실들을 말해 주셨어요. 대왕 갑오징어는 초록색 피를 가지고 있어요. 바닷가재는 파란색 피를 가지고 있고, 100년까지 살아요. 새우는 뒤로만 헤엄칠 수 있어요. 전기 장어는 전구 10개를 밝힐 수 있어요.

이런 재미있는 사실들은 우리가 그 동물들을 쉽게 알아보게 해줬어요. 그것들은 또한 배우기에 재미있었어요!

Comprehension Check　35쪽

A　1. T　그들은 반에서 바다 동물들을 공부하고 있어요.
　　2. F　학생들은 TV 프로그램에서 바다 동물들을 봤어요.
　　3. T　새우는 뒤로만 헤엄칠 수 있어요.

B　1. ⓒ 이 지문은 주로 바다 동물들에 대한 거예요.
　　　　ⓐ 어부들　ⓑ 바다사자들
　　2. ⓒ 어느 바다 동물이 초록색 피를 가졌나요?
　　　　ⓐ 해파리　ⓑ 바닷가재　ⓒ 대왕 갑오징어
　　3. ⓐ 전기 장어에 대한 것 중 사실인 것은 무엇인가요?
　　　　ⓐ 그들은 전구 10개를 밝힐 수 있어요.
　　　　ⓑ 그들은 뒤로만 헤엄칠 수 있어요.
　　　　ⓒ 그들은 100년까지 살 수 있어요.

C　1. pictures　왓슨 선생님은 많은 바다 동물들의 사진들을 수업에 가져오셨어요.
　　2. remember　우리는 그것들의 이름 중 몇 개는 알았지만, 그것들 모두를 기억하는 것은 어려웠어요.
　　3. Lobsters　바닷가재는 파란색 피를 가지고 있고, 100년까지 살아요.

Read and Understand　36쪽

1. 많은 바다 동물들의 사진들을
2. 그것들의 이름을 말하는 것을
3. 기타 등등

4. 그것들 모두를 기억하는 것은
5. 각각의 바다 동물에 대한
6. 초록색 피를
7. 100년까지
8. 뒤로만 헤엄친다
9. 전기 장어들은 밝힐 수 있다
10. 우리가 알아보게 해줬다
11. 그것들은 또한 재미있었다

Grammar Point　37쪽

1. 농구를 하는 것은 재미있다.
2. 쿠키를 굽는 것은 어려웠다.

Workbook

A

1. 가져왔다
2. 칠판, 판자
3. 장어
4. 바닷가재
5. 새우
6. 조개
7. 해파리
8. 뒤로
9. 전기의
10. 알아보다

B

1. ⓑ
2. ⓒ
3. ⓓ
4. ⓐ
5. ⓔ
6. ⓗ
7. ⓕ
8. ⓖ
9. ⓘ
10. ⓙ

C

1. brought
2. board
3. name
4. on
5. remember
6. fun
7. blood
8. up to
9. backwards
10. light
11. identify
12. learn

영화 죠스, E.T., 쥬라기 공원을 본 적이 있나요? 스티븐 스필버그는 이 영화들을 모두 감독했어요. 그는 지난 40년 동안 할리우드에서 가장 크게 성공한 영화들 중 많은 작품들을 제작했어요. 그는 그의 영화에 공상 과학, 인본주의, 모험과 같은 다양한 주제와 장르를 사용했어요. 스필버그의 영화는 동적이고 환상적인 장면들을 담고 있었어요. 관중들은 그의 영화에 매우 감명을 받았고 그 영화들을 보면서 무척 재미있어 했어요.

스티븐 스필버그는 1946년 미국 오하이오 주에서 태어났어요. 어린 시절부터 그는 상상력이 뛰어났고 호기심으로 가득했어요. 그는 열두 살에 첫 번째 영화를 촬영했어요. 그 영화는 친구들과 가족들에게 좋은 반응을 받았어요. 요즘에도 스필버그는 훌륭한 영화를 만들기 위해 여전히 열심히 일해요. 그는 자신의 일을 사랑하고 "나는 먹고 살기 위해 꿈을 꾼다"라고 말했어요.

Comprehension Check　39쪽

A 1. T　스티븐 스필버그는 할리우드에서 가장 크게 성공한 영화들 중 많은 작품들을 제작했어요.
　 2. F　스필버그는 연기하는 것과 짧은 노래 만들기를 좋아했어요.
　 3. T　스필버그는 그의 영화에 다양한 장르를 사용했어요.

B 1. ⓐ 이 지문은 주로 <u>스티븐 스필버그</u>에 대한 거예요.
　　 ⓑ 블록버스터들　ⓒ 할리우드
　 2. ⓑ 영화 죠스, 이티, 쥬라기 공원은 크게 성공했어요. 이들을 "<u>블록버스터</u>"라고 불러요.
　　 ⓐ 주제들　ⓒ 모험들
　 3. ⓐ 그는 몇 살에 그의 첫 번째 영화를 촬영했나요?
　　 ⓐ 12살　ⓑ 13살　ⓒ 20살

C 1. impressed, fun　관중들은 그의 영화에 매우 <u>감명을 받</u>았고 그 영화들을 보면서 무척 <u>재미있어</u> 했어요.
　 2. curiosity　어린 시절부터 그는 상상력이 뛰어났고 <u>호기심</u>으로 가득했어요.
　 3. dream　그는 자신의 일을 사랑하고 "나는 먹고 살기 위해 <u>꿈을 꾼다</u>"라고 말했어요.

Read and Understand　40쪽

1. 본 적이 있는가?
2. 이 영화들 모두를

3. 지난 40년 동안
4. 공상 과학, 인본주의, 그리고 모험 같은
5. 동적이고 환상적인 장면들을
6. 관중들은 매우 감명 받았다
7. 태어났다
8. 그는 상상력이 풍부했다
9. 그는 그의 첫 번째 영화를 촬영했다
10. 그것은 좋은 반응을 받았다
11. 훌륭한 영화들을 만들기 위해
12. 나는 먹고 살기 위해 꿈을 꾼다

Grammar Point　41쪽

1. 내 우산 본 적 있어?
2. 새로 온 학생에 대해 들어 봤어?

Workbook

A

1. 제작하다
2. 모험
3. 영화; 촬영하다
4. 담고 있다
5. 활동적인
6. 환상적인
7. 관중, 청중
8. 상상
9. 호기심
10. 꿈; 꿈을 꾸다

B

1. ⓐ
2. ⓓ
3. ⓔ
4. ⓒ
5. ⓑ
6. ⓗ
7. ⓕ
8. ⓖ
9. ⓘ
10. ⓙ

C

1. seen
2. all
3. many
4. over
5. fiction
6. contained
7. impressed
8. watching
9. imagination
10. curiosity
11. at
12. living

커다란 돌 안에 검이 있었어요. 그 돌에는 이런 글이 있었어요. "오직 왕만이 돌에서 검을 뽑을 수 있다." 모든 기사들이 돌에서 검을 뽑으려고 노력했어요. 그들은 잡아당기고 또 잡아당겼지만, 아무도 돌에서 검을 빼낼 수 없었어요.

나라에서 큰 마상시합이 있었어요. 많은 기사들이 와서 말을 타고 손에 검을 든 채 싸웠어요. 열다섯 살 소년인 아더 역시 다른 기사들과 함께 싸우고 싶었어요. 하지만 아더에게는 검이 없었어요.

아더는 돌을 향해 갔어요. 그는 검을 손에 쥐고 잡아당겼어요. 그것은 돌 밖으로 쉽게 빠져나왔어요. 아더 주위에 군중이 모였어요. 그 군중은 환호했고, 아더는 영국의 왕위에 올랐어요.

Comprehension Check
43쪽

A 1. F 커다란 상자 안에 검이 있었어요.
   2. F 오직 기사만이 돌에서 검을 뽑을 수 있었어요.
   3. T 열다섯 살에 아더는 돌에서 검을 빼냈어요.

B 1. ⓐ 이 지문은 주로 돌에 있는 검에 대한 거예요.
     ⓑ 기사들의 검   ⓒ 영국의 기사들
   2. ⓒ 기사들이 마상시합에 와서 말을 타고 검을 든 채 싸웠어요.
     ⓐ 전쟁   ⓑ 축제
   3. ⓑ 아더가 돌에서 검을 뽑은 후에 어떤 일이 벌어졌나요?
     ⓐ 그는 큰 마상시합에 참여했어요.
     ⓑ 그는 영국의 왕이 되었어요.
     ⓒ 그는 왕의 기사가 되었어요.

C 1. king "오직 왕만이 돌에서 검을 뽑을 수 있다."
   2. pull 모든 기사들이 돌에서 검을 뽑으려고 노력했어요.
   3. crowned 아더는 영국의 왕위에 올랐어요.

Read and Understand
44쪽

1. 커다란 돌 안에
2. 검을 뽑을[가져갈] 수 있다
3. 검을 뽑으려고 노력했다
4. 하지만 아무도 그것을 뽑을 수 없었다
5. 큰 마상시합이 있었다
6. 손에 검을 들고
7. 다른 기사들과 함께

8. 그는 검이 없었다
9. 돌을 향해
10. 그의 손에
11. 그것은 돌에서 빠져나왔다
12. 아더 주위에 모인
13. 그리고 아더는 왕위에 올랐다

Grammar Point
45쪽

1. 다음에 무슨 일이 일어날지는 아무도 모른다.
2. 아무것도 우리를 막을 수 없다.

Workbook

A

1. 검
2. 돌
3. (중세의) 기사
4. 뽑다, 당기다
5. 나라
6. 싸웠다
7. 싸우다
8. 군중
9. 모이다
10. 왕위에 앉히다

B

1. ⓓ
2. ⓐ
3. ⓒ
4. ⓔ
5. ⓑ
6. ⓗ
7. ⓘ
8. ⓕ
9. ⓙ
10. ⓖ

C

1. sword
2. KING
3. pull
4. nobody
5. tournament
6. fought
7. knights
8. took
9. easily
10. crowd
11. crowned

사람들이 화성에서 살 수 있을까요? 아마도 언젠가는요. 로버는 NASA에 의해 개발된 로봇이에요. 이 로봇들은 화성의 표면을 탐사하고 과학적인 자료를 수집해요. 로버들은 우리가 화성에 대해 알도록 도와줘요. 그들은 로봇 과학자와 같아요.

로버들은 고대 생명체의 흔적을 찾기 위해 암석과 토양을 연구해요. 그들은 또한 화성에서 날씨도 확인해요. 이것은 사람들이 아마도 화성에 갈 수 있는 미래의 여행을 위해 중요해요. 로버들은 화성이 인간에게 안전한지 알아보는 데 도움을 줘요. 그들은 또한 물 같은 유용한 것들도 찾아요. 그들은 과학자들이 사람들을 위한 안전한 집과 도구를 만들도록 도와줘요. 화성에 대해 더 많이 아는 것은 사람들이 그곳에서 사는 것을 더 쉬워지게 만들어요.

로버들 덕분에 언젠가 화성에서 사는 꿈이 이루어질 수도 있어요!

Comprehension Check 47쪽

A 1. F 로버는 고대 사람들에 의해 개발되었다.
   2. T 로버는 화성에서 날씨를 확인할 수 있다.
   3. T 로버는 미래의 여행을 위해 중요하다.

B 1. ⓑ 이 지문은 대체로 나사의 로버가 우리가 화성을 이해하는 데 어떻게 도움을 주는지에 대한 거예요.
      ⓐ 나사가 우리에게 얼만큼 도움을 주는지
      ⓒ 화성 여행이 얼마나 즐거운지
   2. ⓐ 로버가 화성에서 고대 생명체의 흔적을 찾기 위해 무엇을 연구하나요?
      ⓐ 그들은 고대 생명체의 흔적을 찾기 위해 암석과 토양을 연구해요.
      ⓑ 그들은 고대 생명체의 흔적을 찾기 위해 로봇을 연구해요.
      ⓒ 그들은 고대 생명체의 흔적을 찾기 위해 인간을 연구해요.
   3. ⓒ 로버가 화성에서 물과 같이 유용한 것들을 찾아내는 게 왜 중요한가요?
      ⓐ 과학자들이 암석을 찾는 데 도움을 주기 때문에.
      ⓑ 과학자들이 댐을 만드는 데 도움을 주기 때문에.
      ⓒ 과학자들이 사람을 위한 안전한 집과 도구를 만드는 데 도움을 주기 때문에.

C 1. surface, scientific 로버는 화성의 표면을 탐험하고 과학적인 자료를 수집해요.
   2. trips 이것은 사람들이 아마도 화성에 갈 수 있는 미래 여행에 중요해요.
   3. Mars, live 화성에 대해 더 많이 아는 것은 사람들이 그곳에서 사는 것을 더 쉬워지게 만들어요.

Read and Understand 48쪽

1. 사람들이 살 수 있을까/언젠가 2. NASA에 의해 개발된
3. 화성의 표면을/과학적인 자료를
4. 로버들은 우리를 돕는다 5. 로봇 과학자들과 같은
6. 고대 생명체의 흔적을 찾기 위해
7. 그들은 또한 확인한다 8. 미래의 여행을 위해
9. 화성이 안전한지 10. 유용한 것들을
11. 사람들을 위한 안전한 집들과 도구들을
12. 화성에 대해 더 많이 아는 것은 13. 화성에서 사는 꿈은

Grammar Point 49쪽

1. 규칙적으로 운동하는 것이 건강을 유지하는 것을 더 쉽게 만들어 준다.
2. 새로운 언어를 배우는 것은 여행자들이 의사소통하는 것을 더 쉬워지게 만든다.

Workbook

A

1. 개발하다 6. 신호, 징후
2. 탐험하다 7. 고대의
3. 표면 8. ~할지도 모른다
4. 모으다 9. 유용한
5. 과학적인 10. 도구

B

1. ⓒ 6. ⓗ
2. ⓓ 7. ⓘ
3. ⓐ 8. ⓖ
4. ⓔ 9. ⓙ
5. ⓑ 10. ⓕ

C

1. live 7. where
2. someday 8. if
3. by 9. like
4. collect 10. Knowing
5. find 11. easier
6. on 12. to

제리는 삼촌의 과수원에 방문했어요. 다양한 종류의 과일 나무들이 많이 있었어요. 그는 또한 땅에서 많은 과일 씨앗들을 발견했어요. 그것들은 크기, 모양, 그리고 색깔이 모두 달랐어요.

제리는 그것들이 어떤 종류의 씨앗인지 궁금해서 삼촌에게 물어봤어요. 그는 탁구공만큼 큰 씨앗 하나를 집었어요. 그것은 갈색이고 둥근 모양이었어요. 삼촌은 그것이 아보카도 씨앗이라고 말했어요. 그 다음에 제리는 동전 크기인 납작하고 타원형인 씨앗을 들었어요. 그것은 살구 씨앗이었어요.

그는 그가 아는 씨앗 하나를 발견했어요. 그것은 그가 가장 좋아하는 과일의 씨앗이었어요. 그것은 완두콩처럼 생겼고 베이지색이었어요. 맞아요! 그것은 체리 씨앗이었어요.

Comprehension Check 51쪽

A
1. T 과수원에는 다양한 종류의 과일 나무들이 많이 있었어요.
2. F 제리가 가장 좋아하는 과일은 살구예요.
3. T 아보카도 씨앗은 탁구공만큼 커요.

B
1. ⓒ 이 지문은 주로 과일 씨앗에 대한 거예요.
   ⓐ 삼촌의 집 ⓑ 과일 나무들
2. ⓒ 제리가 가장 좋아하는 과일은 무엇이가요?
   ⓐ 아보카도 ⓑ 살구 ⓒ 체리
3. ⓑ 살구씨는 어떻게 생겼나요?
   ⓐ 매우 크고, 갈색이며 둥근 모양이에요.
   ⓑ 납작하고 타원형이며 동전 크기예요.
   ⓒ 완두콩처럼 생겼고 베이지색이에요.

C
1. kinds 다양한 종류의 과일 나무들이 많이 있었어요.
2. ground 제리는 땅에서 많은 과일 씨앗들을 발견했어요.
3. big 그는 탁구공만큼 큰 씨앗 하나를 집었어요.

Read and Understand 52쪽

1. 그의 삼촌의 과수원을
2. 많은 다양한 종류가
3. 많은 과일 씨앗들을
4. 다른 크기, 모양, 그리고 색깔을
5. 그것들이 어떤 종류의 씨앗인지
6. 탁구공만큼 큰
7. 갈색이고 둥근
8. 그것은 아보카도 씨앗이라고
9. 동전 크기인
10. 살구 씨앗
11. 그가 알고 있는
12. 그가 가장 좋아하는 과일의
13. 그것은 완두콩처럼 생겼다

Grammar Point 53쪽

1. 나는 이 치마와 잘 어울리는 모자가 필요하다.
2. 우리는 축구공만큼 큰 빵을 발견했다.

Workbook

A
1. 삼촌
2. 과수원
3. 종류
4. 씨앗
5. 궁금해하다
6. 집어 들다
7. 손에 (들었다)
8. 납작한
9. 타원형
10. 동전

B
1. ⓓ
2. ⓔ
3. ⓐ
4. ⓑ
5. ⓒ
6. ⓘ
7. ⓕ
8. ⓙ
9. ⓗ
10. ⓖ

C
1. orchard
2. were
3. seeds
4. different
5. kind
6. picked
7. as
8. round
9. held
10. size
11. favorite
12. like

추수감사절은 미국에서 11월 넷째 주 목요일에 기념해요. 이는 농작물을 수확하는 날을 기념하는 거예요.

1620년 겨울에, 청교도로 알려진 영국 사람들의 절반이 미국에서 농작물을 수확하는 데 실패해서 굶어 죽었어요. 미국 원주민들은 청교도들에게 농작물을 재배하고 수확하는 방법을 가르쳐 줬어요. 이듬해인 1621년, 청교도들은 농작물 수확에 성공했어요.

청교도들은 성공적인 수확을 기념하기 위해 미국 원주민들을 초대했어요. 청교도들과 미국 원주민들은 옥수수, 콩, 그리고 호박을 먹었어요. 그들은 또한 물고기를 잡아서 함께 먹었어요. 이러한 이유에서 미국인들은 추수감사절을 기념한답니다.

Comprehension Check 57쪽

A 1. T 미국에서 추수감사절은 11월에 기념해요.
2. F 추수감사절은 농작물을 심는 날을 기념하는 거예요.
3. F 청교도들은 미국 원주민들에게 농작물을 재배하는 방법을 가르쳐 줬어요.

B 1. ⓐ 이 지문은 주로 추수감사절에 대한 거예요.
ⓑ 청교도들 ⓒ 농작물 수확하기
2. ⓑ 많은 청교도들이 왜 굶어 죽었나요?
ⓐ 미국 원주민들이 물고기를 잡아 먹었기 때문에
ⓑ 미국에서 농작물을 수확하는 데 실패했기 때문에
ⓒ 미국 원주민들이 그들에게 농작물을 재배하고 수확하는 방법을 알려줬기 때문에
3. ⓐ 청교도들은 왜 축제에 미국 원주민들을 초대했나요?
ⓐ 성공적인 수확을 기념하기 위해서
ⓑ 함께 영국을 여행하기 위해서
ⓒ 농작물을 재배하고 수확하기 위해서

C 1. fourth, November 추수감사절은 미국에서 11월 넷째 주 목요일에 기념해요.
2. succeeded 이듬해인 1621년, 청교도들은 농작물 수확에 성공했어요.
3. pumpkins 청교도들과 미국 원주민들은 옥수수, 콩, 그리고 호박을 먹었어요.

Read and Understand 58쪽

1. 네 번째 목요일에

2. 농작물을 수확하는 날로
3. 굶어 죽었다
4. 농작물을 재배하고 수확하는 방법을
5. 청교도들은 성공했다
6. 성공적인 수확을
7. 옥수수, 콩, 그리고 호박을
8. 그리고 그것들을 함께 먹었다
9. 이것이 ~하는 이유이다

Grammar Point 59쪽

1. 내가 도착했을 때 그들은 점심을 다 먹었었다.
2. 내가 여기로 이사 오기 전에 그녀가 이 집에서 살았었다.

Workbook

A
1. 기념하다
2. 11월
3. 수확하다; 수확
4. 농작물
5. 굶주리다
6. 실패하다
7. 성공하다
8. 초대하다
9. 성공적인
10. 호박

B
1. ⓐ
2. ⓔ
3. ⓓ
4. ⓒ
5. ⓑ
6. ⓗ
7. ⓕ
8. ⓖ
9. ⓙ
10. ⓘ

C
1. on
2. is celebrated
3. half
4. known
5. death
6. had failed
7. how
8. succeeded
9. successful
10. ate
11. fish
12. why

큐피드는 로마의 사랑의 신이었어요. 그는 그리스어로 에로스라고 불리기도 했어요. 그는 사랑과 미의 여신인 비너스의 아들이었어요.

큐피드와 그의 화살에 대한 신화들이 있었어요. 큐피드의 화살은 당신을 사랑에 빠지게 만들 수 있어요. 큐피드는 등에 날개가 있어서 날 수 있었어요. 그는 활과 두 종류의 화살을 가지고 다녔어요. 한 종류는 날카로운 금 화살촉이 있었고, 다른 한 종류는 뭉툭한 납 화살촉이 있었어요.

큐피드가 금 화살로 사람을 쏘면, 그 사람은 바로 다음에 보는 사람과 사랑에 빠졌어요. 하지만 큐피드가 누군가를 납 화살로 쏘면, 이 사람은 다음에 보는 사람을 증오했어요.

그러니 조심하세요! 큐피드가 언젠가는 여러분을 쏠 수도 있어요.

Comprehension Check 61쪽

A 1. F 비너스는 로마의 사랑의 신이었어요.
2. T 큐피드는 활과 두 종류의 화살을 가지고 다녔어요.
3. F 큐피드가 납 화살로 사람을 쏘면, 이 사람은 누군가와 사랑에 빠졌어요.

B 1. b 이 지문은 주로 큐피드의 화살들에 대한 거예요.
ⓐ 로마 사람들 ⓒ 사랑에 빠지는 것
2. c 어느 화살이 바로 다음에 보는 사람을 증오하게 만들었나요?
ⓐ 금 화살 ⓑ 초록색 화살 ⓒ 납 화살
3. b 이야기에 비춰볼 때 큐피드에 대해 옳은 것은?
ⓐ 큐피드는 제우스로부터 화살을 훔쳤어요.
ⓑ 큐피드의 등에는 날개가 있었어요.
ⓒ 비너스는 큐피드의 아들이었어요.

C 1. Eros 큐피드는 그리스어로 에로스라고 불리기도 했어요.
2. golden, love 큐피드가 금 화살로 사람을 쏘면, 그 사람은 바로 다음에 보는 사람과 사랑에 빠졌어요.
3. out, shoot 그러니 조심해요! 큐피드가 언젠가는 여러분을 쏠 수도 있어요.

Read and Understand 62쪽

1. 로마의 신
2. 그리스어로
3. 사랑과 미의 여신인
4. 신화들이 있었다
5. 사랑에 빠지게
6. 그의 등에
7. 활과 두 종류의 화살을
8. 뭉툭한 납 화살촉을
9. 바로 다음 사람과
10. 큐피드가 누군가를 쏘면
11. 큐피드가 당신을 쏠지도 모른다

Grammar Point 63쪽

1. 하나는 검정색이고, 다른 하나는 파란색이다.
2. 한 컵에는 우유가 있고, 다른 컵에는 주스가 있다.

Workbook

A
1. 로마의
2. 신
3. 그리스어
4. 여신
5. 아름다움
6. 신화
7. 화살
8. 활
9. 쐈다
10. 쏘다

B
1. c
2. e
3. d
4. b
5. a
6. g
7. f
8. i
9. h
10. j

C
1. god
2. Greek
3. goddess
4. myths
5. back
6. sharp
7. blunt
8. golden
9. very
10. lead
11. hated
12. might

All About Fish | 물고기에 대한 모든 것

물고기는 평생을 물속에서 보내요. 32,000종의 다양한 물고기가 있어요. 어떤 물고기들은 길이가 2,700cm나 되고, 어떤 물고기들은 길이가 8mm밖에 안 돼요.

물고기는 살기 위해서 사람처럼 산소가 필요해요. 사람은 공기를 호흡하기 위해 허파를 가지고 있지만, 물고기는 아가미를 가지고 있어요. 아가미는 물고기가 물속에서 호흡하도록 도와줘요.

사람처럼 물고기도 잠을 자요. 물고기는 눈꺼풀이 없기 때문에 눈을 뜬 채로 잠을 자요. 하지만 항상 예외가 있어요. 어떤 상어들은 눈꺼풀이 있어요. 하지만 그들은 눈을 뜬 채로 잠을 자요. 만약 여러분이 느리게 움직이는 물고기를 보면, 그것은 잠을 자고 있는지도 몰라요. 대부분의 물고기는 산소를 호흡해야 하기 때문에 잠을 잘 때 움직여요.

Comprehension Check — 65쪽

A 1. T 물고기는 평생을 물속에서 보내요.
  2. T 다양한 종의 물고기가 있어요.
  3. F 물고기는 공기를 호흡하기 위해 사람처럼 허파를 가지고 있어요.

B 1. ⓑ 이 지문은 주로 물고기에 대한 거예요.
    ⓐ 물 ⓒ 아가미
  2. ⓑ 물고기들은 왜 눈을 뜬 채로 잠을 자나요?
    ⓐ 물고기는 폐가 없어서
    ⓑ 물고기는 눈꺼풀이 없어서
    ⓒ 물고기는 뇌가 없어서
  3. ⓒ 물고기는 물속에서 어떻게 숨을 쉴 수 있나요?
    ⓐ 물고기는 폐를 통해 호흡해요.
    ⓑ 물고기는 눈꺼풀을 통해 호흡해요.
    ⓒ 물고기는 아가미를 통해 호흡해요.

C 1. Gills 아가미는 물고기가 물속에서 호흡하도록 도와줘요.
  2. sharks 어떤 상어들은 눈꺼풀이 있어요.
  3. sleeping 만약 여러분이 느리게 움직이는 물고기를 보면, 그것은 잠을 자고 있는지도 몰라요.

Read and Understand — 66쪽

1. 그들의 평생을
2. 32,000개의 다양한 종이
3. 길이가 2,700cm까지
4. 살기 위해서
5. 공기를 호흡하기 위해
6. 물속에서
7. 사람들처럼
8. 그들의 눈을 뜬 채로
9. 항상 예외가
10. 눈꺼풀이 있다
11. 그것은 자고 있는지도 모른다
12. 그들이 자고 있을 때

Grammar Point — 67쪽

1. 그는 손을 주머니에 넣은 채 걷는다.
2. 그녀는 입을 가린 채 웃는다.

Workbook

A
1. (시간을) 보내다
2. 전체의
3. (생물) 종
4. 인간, 사람
5. 허파
6. 아가미
7. 눈꺼풀
8. 항상
9. 예외
10. 상어

B
1. ⓓ
2. ⓐ
3. ⓔ
4. ⓑ
5. ⓒ
6. ⓗ
7. ⓙ
8. ⓕ
9. ⓖ
10. ⓘ

C
1. lives
2. species
3. fish
4. others
5. lungs
6. gills
7. breathe
8. Like
9. with
10. eyelids
11. open
12. because

제니는 방에 크고 지저분한 옷장이 있었어요. 제니는 그 옷장 안에 자신의 모든 물건들을 넣는 것을 좋아했어요. 그녀는 자기의 옷들, 모자들, 양말들, 가방들, 인형들, 머리핀들, 그리고 심지어 신발들까지 옷장 안에 넣었어요. 제니의 엄마는 항상 그녀에게 옷장을 깨끗이 치우라고 말했어요. 하지만 제니는 그 상태 그대로가 좋았어요.

어느 날, 제니는 친구의 생일파티에 초대받았어요. 그녀는 보라색 셔츠를 입고 싶었지만, 찾을 수가 없었어요. 제니는 허리를 구부려 마침내 옷장의 뒤쪽에서 그 셔츠의 일부를 발견했어요. 제니는 그것을 힘껏 잡아당겼어요. 갑자기 셔츠와 함께 모든 것들이 나왔어요. 제니는 물건들 아래에 묻혔고, 보라색 셔츠는 찢어졌어요.

"앞으로는 절대 옷장을 지저분하게 두지 않을 거야."

Comprehension Check   69쪽

A 1. T   제니는 옷장에 자신의 모든 물건을 넣는 것을 좋아했어요.
   2. F   제니는 엄마에게 항상 옷장을 깨끗이 치우라고 말했어요.
   3. F   제니의 보라색 셔츠는 옷장에 없었어요.

B 1. ⓒ 이 지문은 주로 <u>지저분한 옷장</u>에 대한 거예요.
     ⓐ 보라색 셔츠   ⓑ 제니와 그녀의 엄마
   2. ⓐ 제니는 왜 보라색 셔츠를 입고 싶어 했나요?
     ⓐ 친구의 생일파티에 초대받았기 때문에
     ⓑ 학교에 가야만 했기 때문에
     ⓒ 조부모님 댁을 방문하고 싶었기 때문에
   3. ⓑ 제니의 보라색 셔츠는 어떻게 되었나요?
     ⓐ 세탁기로 세탁되었어요.
     ⓑ 찢어졌어요.
     ⓒ 옷장에 없었어요.

C 1. even 그녀는 그녀의 옷들, 모자들, 양말들, 가방들, 인형들, 머리핀들, 그리고 <u>심지어</u> 신발들까지 그 안에 넣었어요.
   2. buried, ripped 제니는 물건들 아래에 <u>묻혔</u>고, 보라색 셔츠는 찢어졌어요.
   3. never 앞으로는 절대 옷장을 지저분하게 두지 <u>않을</u> 거야.

Read and Understand   70쪽

1. 크고 지저분한 옷장을
2. 그녀의 모든 물건들을

3. 그리고 심지어 신발들까지
4. 옷장을 깨끗이 치우라고
5. 그 상태 그대로
6. 제니는 초대받았다
7. 그녀의 보라색 셔츠를
8. 그리고 마침내 발견했다
9. 그것을 세게 잡아당겼다
10. 모든 것이 나왔다
11. 찢어졌다
12. 앞으로는

Grammar Point   71쪽

1. 의사는 나에게 침대에서 쉬라고 말했다.
2. 나는 그에게 오늘 나한테 전화하라고 말했다.

Workbook

A

1. 지저분한
2. 옷장
3. 물건
4. 굽혔다
5. 마침내
6. 일부, 부품
7. 뒤쪽
8. (보이지 않게) 묻다
9. 찢다
10. 앞으로는

B

1. ⓒ
2. ⓓ
3. ⓑ
4. ⓔ
5. ⓐ
6. ⓖ
7. ⓘ
8. ⓕ
9. ⓙ
10. ⓗ

C

1. messy
2. stuff
3. even
4. out
5. was invited
6. bent
7. back
8. hard
9. buried
10. ripped
11. on
12. never

물, 바람, 그리고 얼음은 땅을 닳아 없애요. 이것은 침식이라고 불려요. 침식은 바람, 물, 얼음, 그리고 중력에 의해 암석과 흙이 없어지는 거예요. 침식은 지구의 표면을 변화시켜요. 이것은 산꼭대기, 계곡, 해안선을 변화시킬 수 있어요. 침식은 빠르게 일어날 수도 있고, 수천 년이 걸릴 수도 있어요.

폭풍우가 온 뒤에 개울과 호수가 왜 진흙탕이 되는지 알고 있나요? 이것은 침식이 발생하고 있다는 표시예요. 폭풍우는 풍경을 변화시켜요.

바람은 특히 건조한 지역에서 침식을 일으켜요. 바람은 모래, 가벼운 암석, 그리고 자갈을 들어 올려 휩쓸어 가요. 바람 역시 풍경을 변화시켜요. 얼음은 추운 지역에서 침식을 일으켜요. 빙하라고 불리는 거대한 얼음 강은 천천히 움직이며 계곡과 산을 변화시켜요.

Comprehension Check   73쪽

A   1. T   침식은 지구의 표면을 변화시켜요.
    2. F   침식은 항상 빠르게 발생해요.
    3. F   바람은 특히 추운 지역에서 침식을 일으켜요.

B   1. ⓒ 이 지문은 주로 침식에 대한 거예요.
      ⓐ 중력   ⓑ 지구의 표면
    2. ⓐ 침식을 일으키는 것이 아닌 것은 무엇인가요?
      ⓐ 풍경   ⓑ 얼음   ⓒ 중력
    3. ⓑ 거대한 얼음 강을 무엇이라고 부르나요?
      ⓐ 개울   ⓑ 빙하   ⓒ 해안선

C   1. wear 물, 바람, 그리고 얼음은 땅을 닳아 없애요.
    2. change, peaks 침식은 산꼭대기, 계곡, 해안선을 변화시켜요.
    3. thousands 침식은 빠르게 일어날 수도 있고, 수천 년이 걸릴 수도 있어요.

Read and Understand   74쪽

1. 땅을 닳아 없앤다
2. 암석과 흙을 없애는 것
3. 지구의 표면을
4. 이것은 변화시킬 수 있다
5. 또는 수천 년이 걸릴 수 있다
6. 계곡과 호수가 왜 진흙탕이 되는지

7. 침식이 발생하고 있다는
8. 풍경을
9. 특히 건조한 지역에서
10. 그리고 휩쓸어 간다
11. 바람은 변화시킨다
12. 추운 지역에서
13. 빙하라고 불리는

Grammar Point   75쪽

1. 차가워지기 전에 차를 마시세요.
2. 요즘 우리 개가 살이 찌고 있다.

Workbook

A

1. 침식	6. 진흙투성이인
2. 표면	7. 폭풍우
3. 산꼭대기	8. 풍경
4. 계곡	9. 지역
5. 해안선	10. 자갈

B

1. ⓐ	6. ⓖ
2. ⓒ	7. ⓗ
3. ⓔ	8. ⓕ
4. ⓓ	9. ⓙ
5. ⓑ	10. ⓘ

C

1. wear	7. quickly
2. is called	8. muddy
3. removal	9. sign
4. by	10. causes
5. changes	11. away
6. peaks	12. glaciers

매우 추운 밤이었어요. 성냥팔이 소녀는 집 밖에서 담벼락에 기대고 있었어요. 소녀는 코트도 입지 않고 신발도 신고 있지 않았어요. 소녀는 너무 추웠어요. 소녀는 몸을 따뜻하게 하기 위해 성냥에 불을 붙였어요.

성냥팔이 소녀는 성냥을 들었어요. 그러자 불빛 속에서 따뜻한 난로가 보였어요. 소녀의 발은 따뜻해졌어요. 하지만 성냥이 꺼지자, 난로가 사라져 버렸어요. 소녀는 또 다른 성냥을 켰어요. 소녀는 맛있는 음식으로 가득찬 식탁과 크리스마스 트리가 보였어요. 하지만 성냥은 다시 꺼졌어요.

소녀는 계속해서 성냥에 불을 붙였어요. 이번에는 소녀를 많이 사랑해 주셨던 돌아가신 할머니가 보였어요. 소녀는 할머니를 따라가고 싶었어요.

Comprehension Check 79쪽

A 1. T 성냥팔이 소녀는 추워서 성냥에 불을 붙였어요.
   2. T 소녀는 불빛 속에서 따뜻한 난로가 보였어요.
   3. F 소녀는 집 밖에 크리스마스 트리가 있었어요.

B 1. ⓑ 이 지문은 주로 성냥들을 가지고 있었던 한 소녀에 대한 거예요.
       ⓐ 매우 추운 밤 ⓒ 크리스마스 트리
   2. ⓐ 성냥팔이 소녀가 첫 번째 성냥을 켰을 때, 무엇을 봤나요?
       ⓐ 따뜻한 난로 ⓑ 그녀의 돌아가신 할머니
       ⓒ 맛있는 음식이 가득한 식탁과 크리스마스 트리
   3. ⓒ 이야기에 따르면 무엇이 옳은가요?
       ⓐ 그녀는 할머니와 함께 살아요.
       ⓑ 그녀는 많은 양초들을 가지고 있었어요.
       ⓒ 그녀는 코드를 입지 않았어요.

C 1. leaning 성냥팔이 소녀는 집 밖에서 담벼락에 기대고 있었어요.
   2. lit 소녀는 계속해서 성냥에 불을 붙였어요.
   3. follow 소녀는 할머니를 따라가고 싶었어요.

Read and Understand 80쪽

1. 아주 추운 밤이었다
2. 기대고 있었다

3. 코트도 신발도
4. 자신을 따뜻하게 하기 위해
5. 성냥을 들었다
6. 따뜻했다
7. 그 난로는 사라졌다
8. 또 다른 성냥을
9. 맛있는 음식으로 가득 찬
10. 그 성냥은 꺼졌다
11. 그녀는 계속해서 불을 붙였다
12. 그녀의 돌아가신 할머니를
13. 그녀는 따라가고 싶었다

Grammar Point 81쪽

1. 너 자신을 탓하지 마.
2. 나는 그 파티에서 즐거웠다.

Workbook

A
1. 성냥
2. 기대다
3. ~에 대고, 기대어
4. 담, 벽
5. 불을 붙였다
6. 난로
7. (불이) 꺼졌다
8. 사라진, 떠난
9. (성냥을) 그었다
10. 계속해서

B
1. ⓔ
2. ⓓ
3. ⓒ
4. ⓐ
5. ⓑ
6. ⓖ
7. ⓙ
8. ⓗ
9. ⓘ
10. ⓕ

C
1. against
2. wasn't
3. lit
4. herself
5. held
6. were
7. gone
8. struck
9. table
10. out
11. continuously
12. follow

3D 프린터는 일반적인 프린터와는 달라요. 종이 한 장에 단순한 글자를 출력하는 대신, 3D 프린터는 실제 물건을 출력할 수 있어요! 3D 프린터는 플라스틱, 금속, 종이, 고무, 실리콘 같은 원재료나, 물건을 출력하는 데 필요한 다른 종류의 재료를 분사하거나 짜내요. 악기, 사람의 신체 기관, 신발, 자동차, 그리고 심지어 집 같은 3차원 물체들이 3D 프린터로 만들어질 수 있어요.

요즘에는 많은 다양한 종류의 3D 프린터들이 있어요. 유감스럽게도, 이 프린터들은 대부분의 개인이 구입해서 집에서 사용하기에는 아직 너무 비싸요. 하지만 의류부터 신체 기관까지 모든 것을 만들어 내는 3D 프린터와 함께라면 3D 출력 기술의 미래는 밝은 것 같아요.

Comprehension Check　83쪽

A 1. F　3D 프린터는 종이 한 장에 글자를 출력해요.
　 2. T　사람들은 3D 프린터로 인간의 신체 기관들을 만들었어요.
　 3. F　요즘 3D 프린터의 종류는 한 가지뿐이에요.

B 1. ⓑ 이 지문은 주로 3D 프린터에 대한 거예요.
　　　ⓐ 일반 프린터들　ⓒ 종이 한 장을 출력하는 것
　 2. ⓐ 3D 프린터는 물건을 어떻게 프린트 하나요?
　　　ⓐ 원자재를 분사하거나 짜내서
　　　ⓑ 종이에 단순한 글자들을 출력해서
　　　ⓒ 재료들을 자르고 풀 붙여서
　 3. ⓒ 너무 비싸기 때문에, 개인들은 3D 프린터를 사서 집에서 사용할 수 없어요.
　　　ⓐ 너무 무거워서　ⓑ 너무 복잡해서

C 1. regular 3D 프린터는 일반적인 프린터와는 달라요.
　 2. Instead, real 종이 한 장에 단순한 글자를 출력하는 대신, 3D 프린터는 실제 물건을 출력할 수 있어요!
　 3. creating, bright 의류부터 신체 기관까지 모든 것을 만들어 내는 3D 프린터와 함께라면 3D 출력 기술의 미래는 밝은 것 같아요.

Read and Understand　84쪽

1. 일반적인 프린터
2. 종이 한 장에
3. 또는 다른 종류의 재료를

4. 만들어질 수 있다
5. 많은 다양한 종류의 3D 프린터들이
6. 구입해서 집에서 사용하기에는
7. 미래는 밝은 것 같다

Grammar Point　85쪽

1. 여기 내가 갖고 싶어 하는 차가 있다.
2. 저것은 네 할아버지가 심은 소나무이다.

Workbook

A
1. 글자
2. 실제의, 진짜의
3. 짜내다
4. 재료
5. 플라스틱
6. 금속
7. 고무
8. 물체
9. 개인
10. 기술

B
1. ⓑ
2. ⓓ
3. ⓔ
4. ⓐ
5. ⓒ
6. ⓗ
7. ⓙ
8. ⓕ
9. ⓖ
10. ⓘ

C
1. regular
2. real
3. materials
4. is needed
5. out
6. objects
7. made
8. these
9. expensive
10. individuals
11. However
12. bright

스테이시는 학교 신문 기자예요. 그녀는 시청에 대한 기사를 쓰고 싶었어요. 스테이시는 생각했어요. "모두 시청이 어디 있는지는 알고 있어. 하지만 그곳에서 어떤 일이 벌어지는지 알고 있을까?"

며칠 후, 스테이시는 재닛 던컨 시장님을 인터뷰했어요. 시장의 사무실은 시청 안에 있었어요.
"여기서 어떤 일을 하시나요?" 스테이시가 물었어요.
"나는 시장으로서 시의회 회의를 이끌죠." 재닛이 말했어요. "우리는 우리 시를 위한 중요한 결정들을 내리기 위해 정기적으로 만나요."
"예를 들어 주시겠어요?" 스테이시가 물었어요.
"음, 어떤 사람이 초등학교 바로 옆에 대형 백화점을 열고 싶어 한다고 상상해 보세요. 많은 쇼핑객들이 학교 근처에서 운전을 할 테니 그것은 위험할 수 있어요. 그러니 우리는 그것을 허가하지 않겠죠."
"와, 그러니까 시장님은 우리 마을을 안전하게 지켜 주시는군요!" 스테이시가 말했어요.

Comprehension Check 87쪽

A 1. F 스테이시는 학교 신문에 대한 기사를 쓰고 싶었어요.
2. T 스테이시는 시장님을 인터뷰했어요.
3. T 시장은 시 의회 회의를 이끌어요.

B 1. ⓒ 이 지문은 주로 시청에서 어떤 일이 벌어지는지에 대한 거예요.
  ⓐ 시청에 누가 사는지 ⓑ 시청이 어디에 있는지
2. ⓐ 스테이시는 왜 시청에 대한 기사를 쓰고 싶었나요?
  ⓐ 거기서 어떤 일이 벌어지는지 알고 싶어서
  ⓑ 누가 거기서 일하는지 알고 싶어서
  ⓒ 시청이 어디에 위치해 있는지 알고 싶어서
3. ⓐ 시장이 마을을 하는 역할들 중 하나는 무엇인가요?
  ⓐ 중요한 결정들을 내리기 위해 시의회 회의를 이끄는 것
  ⓑ 시청 바로 옆에 대형 백화점을 짓는 것
  ⓒ 시청에 대한 기사를 쓰는 것

C 1. reporter 스테이시는 학교 신문 기자예요.
2. happens "모두 시청이 어디 있는지는 알고 있어. 하지만 그곳에서 어떤 일이 벌어지는지 알고 있을까?"
3. dangerous "많은 쇼핑객들이 학교 근처에서 운전을 할 테니 위험할 수 있어요."

Read and Understand 88쪽

1. 학교 신문 기자
2. 기사를 쓰는 것을
3. 시청이 어디에 있는지
4. 그곳에서 어떤 일이 벌어지는지
5. 며칠 후
6. 시장님의 사무실은
7. 스테이시가 물었다
8. 시장으로서
9. 중요한 결정들을 내리기 위해
10. 예를 들어 주시겠어요?
11. 초등학교 바로 옆에
12. 그것은 위험할 수 있어요
13. 우리는 허가하지 않겠죠
14. 우리 마을을 안전하게

Grammar Point 89쪽

1. 그녀는 그 식당이 어디에 있는지 안다.
2. 나는 그가 어디에 사는지 안다.

Workbook

A
1. 신문
2. 기자
3. 인터뷰하다
4. 시장
5. 사무실
6. 이끌다
7. 회의
8. 정기적으로
9. 결정
10. 예

B
1. ⓒ
2. ⓔ
3. ⓓ
4. ⓐ
5. ⓑ
6. ⓙ
7. ⓘ
8. ⓕ
9. ⓗ
10. ⓖ

C
1. reporter
2. knows
3. happens
4. mayor
5. lead
6. regularly
7. decisions
8. example
9. imagine
10. because
11. allow
12. safe

지금 이 순간 여러분이 움직이고 있다는 사실을 알고 있었나요? 맞아요! 한국에서, 여러분 밑에 있는 땅은 거의 시속 1,300킬로미터로 움직이고 있어요! 여러분을 데리고 말이죠!

지구는 돌고 있어요. 매끄러운 탁자에 구슬을 올려 놓으세요. 구슬을 돌리세요. 그것이 바로 지구가 하고 있는 거예요. 물론, 우리는 이 움직임이 느껴지지는 않아요. 우리에게는 태양이 움직이는 것처럼 보여요. 그래서 우리는 아침에는 해가 "뜬다", 밤에는 "진다"고 말하죠. 사실 태양은 움직이지 않아요.

지구에서 우리가 있는 쪽이 태양 쪽으로 움직이면, 우리는 낮이 돼요. 그것이 멀어지면, 우리는 밤이 돼요. 지구가 회전 한 바퀴를 끝내는 데는 24시간이 걸려요. 그래서 하루는 길이가 24시간이랍니다!

Comprehension Check 91쪽

A 1. T 여러분 밑에 있는 땅은 움직이고 있어요.
   2. F 우리는 지구의 움직임을 느껴요.
   3. F 태양이 회전 한 바퀴를 끝내는 데는 24시간이 걸려요.

B 1. ⓑ 이 지문은 주로 지구의 움직임에 대한 거예요.
      ⓐ 낮 ⓒ 태양의 움직임
   2. ⓒ 낮과 밤이 어떻게 생기나요?
      ⓐ 태양이 회전하기 때문에
      ⓑ 태양이 지구 주위를 움직이기 때문에
      ⓒ 지구가 태양 주위를 움직이면서 회전하기 때문에
   3. ⓑ 이야기에 따르면 무엇이 사실인가요?
      ⓐ 지구는 한 바퀴 회전하는 데 24일이 걸려요.
      ⓑ 한국에서는 땅이 거의 시속 1,300킬로미터의 속도로 움직이고 있어요.
      ⓒ 지구가 태양으로부터 멀어져서 회전하면 낮이 돼요.

C 1. doing 그것이 바로 지구가 하고 있는 거예요.
   2. sun 우리에게는 태양이 움직이는 것처럼 보여요.
   3. complete 지구가 회전 한 바퀴를 끝내는 데는 24시간이 걸려요.

Read and Understand 92쪽

1. 여러분이 움직이고 있다는 것을
2. 여러분 밑에 있는 땅은

3. 그것은 여러분을 데리고가고 있다
4. 매끄러운 탁자 위에
5. 지구가 하고 있는 것
6. 이런 움직임을
7. 태양이 움직이고 있는 것
8. 아침에 해가 "뜬다"고
9. 태양은 움직이지 않는다
10. 태양 쪽으로 움직인다
11. 그것이 멀어질 때
12. 회전 한 바퀴를 끝내는 데
13. 그래서 하루 길이가 24시간이다

Grammar Point 93쪽

1. 그게 내가 필요한 것이다.
2. 그게 내가 얘기하고 싶은 것이다.

Workbook

A
1. 아래에
2. 돌다; 회전
3. 구슬
4. 매끄러운
5. 움직임
6. ~인 것 같다
7. (해가) 뜨다
8. (해가) 지다
9. ~쪽으로, ~을 향해
10. 완료하다

B
1. ⓒ
2. ⓓ
3. ⓔ
4. ⓐ
5. ⓑ
6. ⓙ
7. ⓗ
8. ⓖ
9. ⓕ
10. ⓘ

C
1. below
2. hour
3. spinning
4. what
5. movement
6. seems
7. why
8. "sets"
9. daytime
10. night
11. takes
12. spin

로빈 후드는 영국의 셔우드 숲에 사는 남자였어요. 그는 부자들을 도둑질해 가난한 사람들에게 주었어요. 그것은 부자들이 셔우드 숲을 지나가는 것을 두려워하게 만들었어요. 그들은 로빈 후드가 그들을 공격할 거라는 것을 알았어요.

어느 날, 장관은 로빈 후드를 잡고 싶어서 계획을 세웠어요. 그는 마을에서 가장 훌륭한 궁수를 뽑는 대회를 열었어요. 장관은 로빈 후드가 훌륭한 궁수이기 때문에, 그 대회에 올 거라는 것을 알았어요.

녹색 옷을 입은 남자가 1등 상을 위해 활을 쏠 마지막 사람이었어요. 화살이 과녁의 중앙을 관통했고, 다른 두 화살들은 장관의 의자에 꽂혔어요. 그것은 로빈 후드였어요.

Comprehension Check 95쪽

A 1. F 로빈 후드는 미국의 셔우드 숲에 살았어요.
   2. T 로빈 후드는 부자들을 도둑질해 가난한 사람들에게 주었어요.
   3. T 녹색 옷을 입은 남자는 로빈 후드였어요.

B 1. ⓑ 이 지문은 주로 로빈 후드에 대한 거예요.
      ⓐ 대회 ⓒ 셔우드 숲
   2. ⓑ 장관은 왜 가장 훌륭한 궁수를 뽑는 대회를 열었나요?
      ⓐ 부자들을 도둑질하고 싶어서
      ⓑ 로빈 후드를 잡고 싶어서
      ⓒ 1등 상을 타고 싶어서
   3. ⓑ 부자들은 왜 셔우드 숲을 지나는 것을 두려워했나요?
      ⓐ 숲속에 무서운 동물들이 있어서
      ⓑ 로빈 후드가 그들을 공격할까 봐
      ⓒ 장관이 셔우드 숲에 살기 때문에

C 1. sheriff, plan 장관은 로빈 후드를 잡고 싶어서 계획을 세웠어요.
   2. shoot 녹색 옷을 입은 남자가 1등 상을 위해 활을 쏠 마지막 사람이었어요.
   3. bull's eye 화살이 과녁의 중앙을 관통했어요.

Read and Understand 96쪽

1. 셔우드 숲에 사는
2. 가난한 사람들에게
3. 셔우드 숲을 지나가는 것을
4. 로빈 후드가 그들을 공격할 거라는 것을
5. 장관은 잡고 싶었다
6. 최고의 궁수를 뽑는
7. 로빈 후드가 올 거라는 것을
8. 녹색 옷을 입은 남자가
9. 화살이 관통했다
10. 그것은 로빈 후드였다

Grammar Point 97쪽

1. 케빈은 키가 크고 똑똑한 남자이다.
2. 농구를 하고 싶어 하는 남자 아이 5명이 있다.

Workbook

A
1. 도둑질하다
2. 통과하다, 지나가다
3. 공격하다
4. 주 장관
5. 잡다
6. 계획
7. 대회
8. 뽑다, 선택하다
9. 상, 상품
10. 맞혔다

B
1. ⓔ
2. ⓓ
3. ⓐ
4. ⓑ
5. ⓒ
6. ⓗ
7. ⓖ
8. ⓕ
9. ⓙ
10. ⓘ

C
1. who
2. robbed
3. the
4. rich
5. attack
6. sheriff
7. archer
8. competition
9. last
10. first
11. through
12. hit

A 1. 곤충들을 잡기 위해   2. 사용한다 / 그들의 이빨을
    3. 독수리와 같은 어떤 새들은 / 그들의 먹이를 잡기 위해

B 1. Some flowers, like sunflowers, use their stems to track the sun.
    2. Some people, like my neighbors, planted trees to reduce air pollution.

A 1. 시작했다
    2. 기타 연주하는 법을 배우는 것을
    3. 시작했다 / 그녀의 옷장을 청소하는 것을

B 1. A small bird started building a new nest.
    2. An old woman began painting a beautiful landscape.

A 1. 마법의 세계를 빠르게 탐험하도록
    2. 피자 파티에 친구들을 초대하도록
    3. 그 시험을 위해 중요한 교훈을 기억하도록

B 1. His friend's hints let him solve the difficult puzzles faster.
    2. The fun experiments let us discover new things about nature.

A 1. 고양이 한 마리를   2. 밝은 빨간색으로 칠해진
    3. 그는 / 말했다 / 이야기 하나를

B 1. They live in a house which is surrounded by trees.
    2. She received a letter which made her very happy.

A 1. 손님들이 도착했을 때
    2. 내가 중국으로 이사갔을 때
    3. 전화가 울렸을 때

B 1. I feel happy when I listen to music.
    2. The train departed when we arrived at the station.

A 1. 왜 하늘이 파란지
    2. 왜 사람들이 크리스마스를 기념하는지
    3. 왜 새들이 겨울에 남쪽으로 날아가는지

B 1. Do you know why we need to drink water?
    2. Do you know why plants need sunlight?

A 1. 비가 도로를 미끄럽게 만들었기 때문에
    2. 모두가 떠났기 때문에
    3. 우리가 소풍을 갈 예정이기 때문에

B 1. It could be salty because I added too much salt to the soup.
    2. It could be tiring because we have to walk a long distance.

A 1. 수학을 가르치는
    2. 어린이를 돕는
    3. 야구 경기에서 이긴

B 1. She is the kind neighbor who lives next door.
    2. The girl is the singer who sang at the party.

기적의 직독직해 120 words A

기적의 직독직해 시리즈

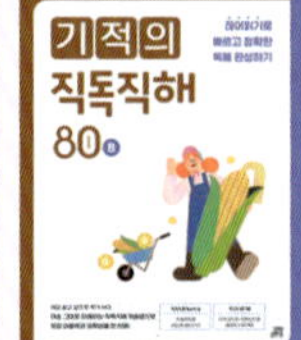

80 words A **80 words B**

초등 고학년 | Lexile 410~600 | AR 2.3~4.3

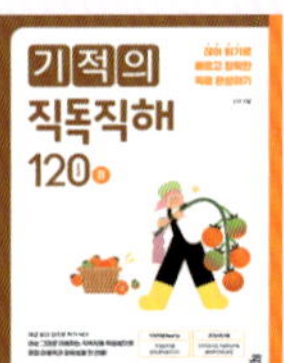

120 words A **120 words B**

예비 중학생 | Lexile 610~800 | AR 3.5~5.2

초등 필수 영어 무작정 따라하기

초등 시기에 놓쳐서는 안 될 필수 학습은 바로 영어 교과서!
영어 교과서 5종의 핵심 내용을 쏙쏙 뽑아 한 권으로 압축 정리했습니다.
초등 과정의 필수학습으로 기초를 다져서 중학교 및 상위 학습의 단단한 토대가 되게 합니다.

| 1~2학년 | 2~3학년 | 2~3학년 | 3학년 이상 | 4학년 이상 |

미국교과서 리딩

문제의 차이가 영어 실력의 차이! 논픽션 리딩에 강해지는 《미국교과서 READING》
논픽션 리딩에 가장 좋은 재료인 미국 교과과정의 주제를 담은 지문을 읽고, 독해력과
문제 해결력을 두루 향상시킬 수 있도록 구성한 단계별 리딩 프로그램

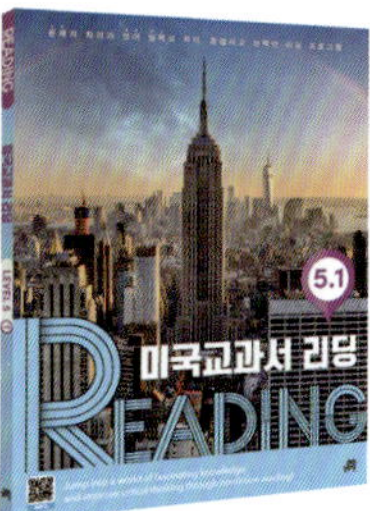

| LEVEL 1 | LEVEL 2 | LEVEL 3 | LEVEL 4 | LEVEL 5 |
| 준비 단계 | 시작 단계 | 정독 연습 단계 | 독해 정확성 향상 단계 | 독해 통합심화 단계 |